P9-CKE-738

HOW TO COACH YOUTH BASEBALL

HOW TO COACH YOUTH BASEBALL

A Step-by-Step Approach

Beverly Breton Carroll

with Fran and Kevin O'Brien

THE LYONS PRESS
Guilford, Connecticut

An imprint of The Globe Pequot Press

To buy books in quantity for corporate use
or incentives, call **(800) 962–0973**
or e-mail **premiums@GlobePequot.com**.

Copyright © 2007 by Beverly Breton Carroll, Francis O'Brien, and Kevin O'Brien

ALL RIGHTS RESERVED. No part of this book may be reproduced or transmitted in any form by any means, electronic or mechanical, including photocopying and recording, or by any information storage and retrieval system, except as may be expressly permitted in writing from the publisher. Requests for permission should be addressed to The Lyons Press, Attn: Rights and Permissions Department, P.O. Box 480, Guilford, CT 06437.

The Lyons Press is an imprint of The Globe Pequot Press.

All interior photos by Matthew Viglianti.

10 9 8 7 6 5 4 3 2 1

Printed in the United States of America

ISBN 978-1-59921-051-3

Library of Congress Cataloging-in-Publication Data is available on file.

CONTENTS

FOREWORD

This book is my opportunity to share with you the knowledge I have gained over the past four decades as a coach on the high school and college levels. I am deeply indebted to the coaches on the college and professional level who have given me the foundation to teach and coach every aspect of the game that I love and respect. It is through them that I have been able to develop individual and team performance that reaches for excellence on the field of play.

It is especially fulfilling for me to share in the book's preparation with my son Kevin. His coaching background and knowledge of the game reflect the multitude of experiences he has had in the game, most recently as part of the Toronto Blue Jays organization.

Most importantly, the expert guidance of Beverly Breton Carroll in coordinating, directing, and enthusiastically supporting our efforts has been much appreciated. Her expertise as a writer and her appreciation for sports and coaching were invaluable in preparing this book.

Lastly, I wish to thank my wife of fifty years, Claire, who has been such a great supporter of my career. It is her love and understanding that has made my coaching experiences a family affair which has been shared with Kevin and his sisters Kathy, Karen, Kelly, and Kristine.

— FRAN O'BRIEN

In the movie *Field of Dreams* Kevin Costner ends up playing catch with Shoeless Joe Jackson, who he figures out is his father. My baseball career has been a living field of dreams as my father and I have enjoyed a tremendous bond fueled by our mutual love for baseball.

Being mentored by one's father is nothing new. Being around a man who is a legendary coach and an extraordinary person is a gift few boys are privileged to experience. My father's personal integrity and care for others supersedes any of his superior coaching. His hallmark as a coach has been his ability to teach, nurture, and instill incredible confidence in his players. His knowledge and feel for the game of baseball is second only to his desire to help people.

Throughout his life he has shared that his goal was to coach in the College World Series. He lived this dream vicariously through his grandson this past June when his grandson Daniel Bard, pitching for the University of North Carolina, stated on national television that his grandfather was his biggest influence in baseball. Daniel called him a baseball genius. My father's love of baseball and influence over young people is truly multigenerational.

Every team has an unsung hero and in our family that would be my mother Claire. She has sacrificed so much to make sure our family was strong and supported in every endeavor. Her devotion and love of her husband and kids is Hall of Fame material.

Having my daughter Khloe be a part of the book as a model for some of the pictures makes this book even more special. I, too, hope to pass on the wonderful game of baseball to my own children. Khloe, Colin, Garret, and Whitney, budding superstars who will get all the love and support they need to become great successes in life, I dedicate this book to you with all my heart.

— KEVIN O'BRIEN

ACKNOWLEDGMENTS

Thank you to my co-authors. Fran, for being the epitome of grace, patience, and baseball knowledge; this book would never have happened without you. Kevin, for supporting the book from the start, and bringing your enthusiasm and love of the game to everything you contributed.

Thanks again to Tom McCarthy. An author couldn't ask for a better editor.

A giant thank you to Mary Jo Rulnick. Author, friend, and former high school softball player, for once more reading every word, then making sure she could act out every drill, never mind if someone at work wondered why she appeared to be pitching an invisible ball or swinging an invisible bat!

A heartfelt thank you to my two favorite go-to guys. My son, Austin, veteran of all-star and high school baseball teams, for willingly demonstrating anything I asked to see, from flat back finish to crow hop. My husband John, former high school baseball player and youth baseball coach, for picking up his cell phone anywhere anytime to answer any question I had about baseball, and for helping me cover all my bases when I was too involved in writing a book on baseball to cover them myself.

And a very special thank you to our models: Connor Green, Ben Johnson, Henri Levenson, Eric McPherson, Khloe O'Brien, Jack Reid, and Ben Richter. You brought such enthusiasm and ability to our photo shoot. Thanks for sharing it!

And may you, and every other person touched by this book, keep enjoying everything baseball offers for many years to come.

— BEVERLY CARROLL

INTRODUCTION

Coaching youth baseball is a wonderful way to share your enthusiasm for a great game while giving back to the young people in your community. You will be an instant role model for the kids on your team, who will look to you for direction on how to become a better player and contribute to a winning team.

Odds are very high that you will not produce a big-leaguer. You will, however, be entrusted to provide a positive experience that imparts such life lessons as teamwork, responsibility, hard work, and respect. As much as the kids will appreciate your knowledge, they will remember how much you cared about them more. Creating a team built on solid values will give the players a strong sense of belonging to a team that has value.

Young players will at times be overcome with emotions in their desire to succeed. They will quickly get discouraged, too. From the beginning, you want them to understand that the goal is to win the game—but not at all costs. More important is that they do their best. Your responsibility as a youth coach is not to win games but to project a winning attitude as an example for your players. Baseball will be a mighty teacher. It humbles even the greatest of players. The most confident young players will have to learn that failure is part of the game; be there for them.

Bringing a team together means being able to handle different personalities with different needs. The image of the youth coach who berates his own players, officials, and the other team remains one that is vivid for many people. But in reality, most youth coaches are mature adults with a proper perspective, a positive attitude, and a desire to promote goodwill on and off the field. You can create an incredible atmosphere for your players to enjoy and learn in. Staying upbeat can be a challenge at times, but keeping in mind the young impressionable minds you have under your tutelage will help you focus.

A very successful pitcher was starting in a crucial game late in the season. He was the most talented player and exuded confidence. His team was relying on him to lead them to the championship, and this game would go a long way to making that happen. By the third inning, the pitcher's inability to get hitters out that day was becoming more and more obvious. Everyone in the order was hitting him hard. The manager went out to the mound and took the pitcher out of the game. The pitcher headed to the corner of the dugout, despondent. He started crying, and quickly put a towel over his head to hide his emotions from his teammates. Seeing this, the coach went over to the pitcher, put his arm around him, consoled him, and gave him an uplifting message to carry him forward. The pitcher was Pedro Martinez and the coach was Willie Randolph of the New York Mets. Even at the highest levels, players need the coach's support.

You will be the maestro who orchestrates the team. It will take some work, but it will bring immeasurable enjoyment to you and your players. What could be a better way to spend time than making kids better players—and better people—by playing the game of baseball?

PART I

THE FUNDAMENTALS

CHAPTER 1

COACHING YOUTH BASEBALL

The other sports are just sports. Baseball is a love.

—BRYANT GUMBEL

Baseball is a love, indeed—a passion shared by millions of people across the fifty states. What's more American than baseball? Walt Whitman called it the American game. And watching it is truly a favorite American pastime.

However, watching a baseball team gets you about as prepared to coach one as eating a gourmet meal gets you prepared to cook one. You've now taken on the glorious responsibility of coaching youth baseball. You have the chance to raise your enjoyment of the sport to a whole new level and to give of yourself to young people at the same time: a win-win proposition, but only if you're prepared.

Practice Breeds Confidence, Confidence Breeds Success

It's important that you and your players are happy to be on the practice field. Only if you feel confident can you make your players feel as though they could conquer anything. Having a plan for practice will foster confidence, enjoyment, improvement, and success—for everyone.

Playing baseball is great fun, but for good reason it has often been called the most difficult game to play. To develop the incredible skill level needed to be successful is a long process. Remind yourself often that this game is full of constant failure. Hitting, for instance, is such a difficult feat that those who fail seven out of ten times are considered a huge success!

Remember, They're Kids

Teaching this sport to younger players takes on added dimensions that you, as a coach, want to keep foremost in your mind. Fielding a ground ball can be a scary proposition to a young player since the ball hurts if it misses his glove and hits him. The embarrassment is worse. As much as you are teaching baseball, you are teaching kids how to handle non-success, peer pressure, parental pressure, and self-image. That is an awful lot for a young person. Your role as a coach should be that of a positive reinforcer finding the silver lining in every setback. As long as the young person is giving a solid effort, improvement will take place. The pace of this improvement varies, but your role is to be a facilitator, bringing out the very best in each kid. Patience, obviously, is a job prerequisite.

Practice Planning 101

Preparing each practice and your series of practices over the season should be an important part of your coaching. While you are not expected to be an expert (that's why you have this guide), your players will respond well to having certain familiar routines. Baseball, in fact, is a sport filled with routines that are taken so seriously players become certain that missing them could seriously affect their game. How about Wade Boggs doing his pregame running at exactly 7:11 P.M. before every game? He's nicknamed "Chicken Man" because his pregame meal had to be chicken. Tales of lucky shirts, socks, and various undergarments worn every day without cleaning for the perceived effect this has on success are legendary. There are thousands of such stories, all bearing testament to the fact that routine is an integral part of baseball—and you want to make it an integral part of practice.

Here's how to get the most out of your practices.

- **Have a written plan.** A written plan will assist you in running a smooth practice and ensure that you cover key areas in preparing your team. Think of it almost as an agenda at a business meeting.

Keep a notebook of your practices. They will be an invaluable reference in the days ahead if you decide to do this for a period of years.

Keep a quick pace. An organized quick-paced practice will keep players interested and leave them invigorated and wanting more. Creating a plan with structure yet flexibility that relates to your players' levels is an asset for any coach, at any level. The more organized you are, the less time you'll waste, and your team will benefit.

Include daily fundamentals. When designing your practice, plan on covering the fundamentals each and every day. This does not mean that you have to spend hours on this, but baseball is a game rooted in the basics. Throwing, catching, hitting, and baserunning should be covered at every practice. Baseball is based on being able to catch consistently and throw accurately. (Sounds simple, right? Go to any youth baseball game in the country and you will see these skills are desperately in need of refinement.)

EXPERIENCE TALKS

Each season, no-hitters are produced in a very limited number. In 1938, Johnny Vander Meer pitched a no-hitter against the Brooklyn Dodgers. This was his second no-hitter in a row. He never pitched another, and this feat has never been duplicated in professional baseball. Coach Fran O'Brien, coaching at Randolph High School in Massachusetts, had the thrill of coaching four consecutive no-hitters! "It sounds impossible," says O'Brien, "but in 1962, Randolph's Barry Needham recorded four no-hitters in a row. As the streak began to unfold, media coverage from Boston newspapers and televisions generated huge crowds. On Barry's attempt for his fifth no-hitter, he was denied by a home run in the third inning with two outs. He had pitched 31 and ⅔ innings without a hit, an accomplishment that may not have been duplicated on that level since."

🔘 **Maintain repetition.** The key to improvement is repetition. Covering the basic fundamentals of the game over and over at every practice will improve each player dramatically and lead to better team play. Adjusting for age and attention span is also critical. Your team may think they've mastered a certain skill and grown out of certain drills, but if the pros haven't grown beyond benefiting from daily drilling, you can bet your team hasn't either.

Build It, and They Will Come

Ultimately, a good coach is a good teacher. Early in the season there is a great deal of teaching, and your teaching tools are the drills. Hitting, fielding, throwing, and pitching win ball games at all levels. If you can improve your players in these areas, you will be a huge success. Every coach must realize that this is a process and takes a great deal of time to master. But build a solid practice plan, take your team through it with liveliness and energy—sharing your pleasure in the game rather than focusing on immediate success—and your kids will come to be better baseball players. You will be rewarded as a coach when you see the novice or mediocre players who wandered onto the field that first practice session become confident solid contributors, game after game.

CHAPTER 2

PRACTICE BASICS

All you have to do is pick up a baseball. It begs to you: Throw me.
— DAVE DRAVECKY

This guide's only presumption is that you like baseball and you have a general idea of how it is played. You may, or may not, have coaching experience. For beginning coaches, you can design and run practices like a pro using this guide. For coaches wanting to expand their abilities, the O'Briens' explanations on why a baseball move is done a certain way and how the move can break down when done incorrectly can help you fine-tune your players' mechanics and understanding of the game.

The drills in each skills chapter are presented in order of the simplest to the most advanced. Terms, moves, and mechanics are generally explained first, followed by a section of *Drills* designed to teach the moves and concepts. Occasionally, a drill offers a *Step It Up* section, which allows you to increase the difficulty of the drill as your players increase their skills. The suggested *Duration* after each drill is how much time to allot during practice to run the drill. The first time you introduce the drill, you want to allow a few more minutes to teach it. Some of the chapters have *Games* that use the skills introduced in the chapter. You can use these when you sense your players need a less structured activity, but they will still be practicing valuable skills.

Before the drill sections, basic equipment and guidelines are introduced, followed by an overview of the drills and games and a system to help you design a practice exactly right for the age and skill level of your players. As you begin to understand the needs of your team and build on your own coaching abilities, you can, of course, begin to modify the suggestions to completely customize your routine. At any point, this guide will allow you to confidently walk onto the diamond, ready to teach and coach your team.

 EXPERIENCE TALKS

With young children, transitioning from drill to drill can be an activity in itself. Leave a little space in your plan. Then, to cover yourself, have a few drills or maybe a game on reserve. If your players move efficiently through the drills, and you have practice time left over, you'll be prepared to add something else. Plan your practices too tight from the start and you're setting yourself up for frustration when your youngsters' capers throw off your schedule.

Equipment Needs

Baseballs

Each team should have two types of baseballs: soft baseballs for certain hitting drills, and regular baseballs for team drills and game-like situations. Because of budget limitations, teach all players to take responsibility for retrieving baseballs on or off the field. You need multiple baseballs to run an efficient practice. Umpires generally require three basically unblemished hard game balls from the home team prior to the first pitch. You also need game balls for pitchers who are warming up in the bullpen and for batting and fielding drills that are part of the regular practice routine. Ideally, your team will have a minimum of three dozen baseballs and three to six dozen soft baseballs to use for practice.

Baseball Buckets

These are large five-gallon plastic buckets to store your baseballs. They are the same as drywall buckets and can be purchased at sporting goods or home improvement stores.

Bases

The traditional game base is a canvas bag secured to the ground with two spikes, but some towns have moved to breakaway bases. The purpose of the breakaway base is to dislodge upon impact in order to prevent sprained or broken ankles. Many towns maintain and set up the fields for games but not for practice, so you will likely need to have a set of bases. For practice sessions, they just need to outline the diamond. Inexpensive, flat, heavy plastic bases are sufficient. In addition, portable plastic home plates to complete the hitting drills and pitching drills are helpful.

Baseball Gloves

Gloves are not provided as part of the team equipment; players provide their own. A glove should be comfortable on the hand and allow for sensitivity to the ball. There are specific glove designs for the different positions. The catcher's glove has extra padding and a claw-like shape. The first baseman's glove is long and wide. Middle infielder gloves are smaller to give players more sensitive handling when fielding and releasing the ball. Third basemen and outfielder gloves are larger so more glove is exposed for catching the ball. Pitchers also have larger gloves to hide the ball from the hitter in the windup, and to protect their bodies and knock line drives to the ground so they can be fielded.

Oiling the glove helps maintain the quality and stability of the leather and can be particularly helpful when breaking in a new glove. Glove oil is available at any sporting goods store. When not in use, oil the glove, place two balls in the pocket, and tie the glove around the balls with a shoelace to help form a glove pocket.

Bats

A team needs a selection of bats varying in length and weight to address the needs of different-sized players. An average Group I (see page 14) level bat would be 24 inches in length and 14 ounces. Group II and III level players would likely be using bats between 28 inches in length, 19 ounces and 32 inches in length, 23 ounces. If a bat is too heavy for a young player, he will not be able to accelerate it through the hitting zone and could get very discouraged. If you see your players picking up bats that are too long or heavy, encourage them to try a different bat. Metal bats continue to be the common bat of choice; however, some leagues and high schools require wooden bats as a safety precaution. Balls come harder and faster off metal bats. Wooden bats are less expensive, but they break much easier, so replacement can be a cost. A *fungoe bat* is also a good practice tool. This is a lighter, narrower, easier-to-swing bat that can be used when multiple balls are being hit by a coach.

EXPERIENCE TALKS

Because of a high school pitcher receiving a near-critical hit in the face from a ball off a metal bat, much discussion was raised in Massachusetts about making wooden bats mandatory in high school. Some high schools began to switch to wooden bats, but many other high school coaches were concerned about the players' abilities to handle bats correctly. When batting with a wooden bat, hitting off the "sweet spot" is critical. Depending on the size of the bat, this spot is a 3- to 5-inch area starting about an inch down from the top of the bat where the ball jumps right off the bat. Ultimately, if a player doesn't get the hang of hitting here, he won't be successful as a hitter. The coaches were concerned that if teams switched to wooden bats, players could get so discouraged about their hitting, they'd switch to another sport! For now, high school leagues mandating wooden bats remain the exception rather than the rule.

Batting Gloves

Players provide their own batting gloves, if desired. They are not necessary equipment, but in colder climates, they can keep players' hands warm earlier in the season. For older players, they protect hands from the wear and tear of repeated practices.

Batting Tees

Teams at all levels should have two appropriately sized batting tees. The batting tees should be adjustable to meet the needs of the hitter based on his size and the drills that are being performed. You may want to reinforce the hitting area with electric tape to protect it from breaking.

Catcher's Gear

Team gear includes the catcher's protective equipment, which is a face mask, chest protector, and shin pads. All the equipment needs to fit properly, so be aware of what size is appropriate for your catchers. Plan to have a backup set of equipment, because if any item is broken during a game, you can't have your catcher out there unprotected or poorly protected.

 EXPERIENCE TALKS A more recent development for catchers is cushioned padding that attaches to the leg and aids the catcher in a crouch position, taking the strain off the knees. These pads are not necessary, but they can make extended practices or games easier on your catcher's legs.

Catcher's Glove

Catchers generally provide their own gloves. Some teams also have a catcher's glove as part of the team equipment for when someone stands in to catch for a pitcher warming up between innings, or for a relief pitcher getting ready to enter a game while the catcher puts on his equipment.

Cleats

T-ball players do not have to have cleats. Above T-ball, players wear cleats. Be aware of your league rules. Some areas ban metal cleats for safety reasons; some mandate designated baseball cleats, which have an extra spike on the front that soccer cleats do not have.

Cones

A smaller version of the type of bright plastic cones used to mark road construction are an important practice supply. Have half a dozen of these to mark measured distances for sprinting and conditioning and certain drills.

Equipment Bags

Oversized equipment bags are a necessity to protect and store equipment. Baseball equipment bags are available, sectioned off for bats and balls, but any large equipment bag will do.

First-Aid Kit

Make sure you have a basic first-aid kit with you at all times. Ice in a plastic bag is best for injuries, but if you use chemical ice packs, come prepared with enough to handle more than one or two injuries per game.

Helmets

All batters are required to wear helmets until they complete their at bat, which includes running the bases. Make this a serious part of games and practices. Helmets on runners are particularly important during team defensive and offensive drills. Your team should have different sizes to adjust to the needs of the players. A helmet should fit relatively snugly on a player's head. Regularly check the helmets for cracks or interior pads that have become unfastened. Helmets take a beating during the course of the season, and it is very easy for them to break down and not provide the safety you're looking for. Each team should have a minimum of six helmets of varying sizes.

Tennis Balls

Each team should have two dozen tennis balls. The tennis balls are used in various drills, particularly catching and hitting drills.

Uniforms

Uniforms are generally provided by your organization. At the younger levels, the players may receive a shirt and hat but need to purchase their own pants, socks, and cleats (if worn). At older levels, pants and socks are also provided. All uniform caps, game socks, and game undershirts are preferably of the same color to complement the uniform.

Field Equipment and Maintenance

Equipment Storage

Ideally, your team has use of a storage area on or near the field. A large locked box that secures the equipment is perfect. However, this type of storage is not available to most teams. Therefore, you want to teach your team that everyone shares the responsibility of gathering the equipment, placing it in designated equipment bags, and carrying it to a vehicle. Practice is not over until the equipment is cared for. This same responsibility holds when you arrive with the equipment; players are to set up and help carry it to the field.

Field Maintenance

You would ideally like to arrive to a practice or game field and find the surface is in pristine condition—but in most cases, this is not reality. Because of weather conditions, lack of maintenance, and, in some cases, general neglect of the field, you will often find the field not ready. To prepare the field, a very basic maintenance kit is a good idea. The kit should consist of a rake, a broom, and a bag of Diamond Dry (a material that absorbs moisture on the field). Make sure the playing surface is clear of rocks and pebbles and debris, the bases are swept, and any puddles are alleviated. An expanded maintenance kit would include three rakes, two brooms, one shovel, Diamond Dry, and mound and home plate tarps.

Protective Screens

Protective batting screens can improve safety with older teams. This batting screen is referred to as an *L screen* because the frame is an L covered with netting to protect the pitcher from batted balls coming back toward the practice mound. This is a piece of equipment that stays at the field, chained to the backstop when not in use.

Number of Coaches and Players

For baseball, you have nine players on the field. Twelve players is an ideal number for most youth teams. If you have too many players, this compromises practice time and game time. But particularly in the younger leagues, you can end up with too few players because of illness or family commitment. If you're coaching a summer league, say, where you know families could be traveling, you may want a roster with a few more players so you never have to forfeit a game due to lack of players.

You can always use the help of assistant coaches for practices and games. For maintaining safe conditions at the youngest level, where kids swing bats and throw baseballs to teammates with rudimentary skills at best, at least one assistant coach is almost imperative. During the game, when your team is at bat, an ideal coaching arrangement is a coach at first, a coach at third, and a coach in the dugout. Older teams may have specialty coaches, for example, a pitching coach and a hitting coach who work consistently with players on just those skills.

Practice Expectations

Group I — Ages 5 and 6

In this group, you are introducing basic fundamentals, rules, and the role of each position player. Focus on teaching the correct skills for catching a ball, throwing a ball, and hitting off a tee, but keep the focus on having fun. Your overall goal is to teach the basics and have each player feel positive about the game of baseball. The practice is no longer than 1½ hours.

Group II — Ages 7 and 8

You are still teaching basic fundamentals to this group: the rules and the role of each position on the field. In addition to working on the correct skills to catch and throw a ball, you are teaching how to hit a pitched ball. You also want to introduce the concept of game tone, urging your players to hustle on and off the field. Encourage more consistent attention from infield and outfield players. Start setting and announcing limited goals for practices and games. Keep the mood positive, and have fun! Players at this level should be starting to understand the mechanics of throwing, catching, and baserunning. The practice is no longer than 1½ hours.

Group III — Ages 9 through 12

A practice focus at this level is on reinforcing individual skill development. These players should be starting to play their positions with some understanding. Introduce the meaning of team play as it relates to offense, defense, and pitching. Begin to increase the goals for practices and games, but be particularly sensitive to the failure factor as it relates to each player. Continue to develop your fielders' ability to concentrate consistently throughout practice and games. Players should hustle on and off the field, keeping game tone constant for the entire game. The pitcher is mastering the strike zone. The catcher is mastering relaying signs from the coach to the pitcher and developing his leadership role. Keep the game fun. Players at this level should be comprehending the game in total and beginning to understand how to adjust to game situations on the field. The practice is no longer than 1¾ hours.

Safety First

Once you have your field and equipment ready, before you start practice, set down some guidelines about general safety.

Safeguarding your players is a critical aspect of coaching baseball. This cannot be stressed enough, for thrown or hit baseballs can be very dangerous—even critical—when players start increasing in size and strength.

"I've always taken time at the beginning to have players understand the impact a bat can have on contact," says Coach Fran O'Brien, "particularly in the facial area. A thrown ball can do equal damage. First and foremost, players need to be aware of the people around them whenever they have a bat or ball in their hands—players or spectators. Secondly, in all my years of coaching, I never stood behind a pair of players warming up. This is a good guideline for everyone to follow. There is always the possibility of a missed ball."

When you organize your drills for practice, also take into consideration the safety of the different groups. Younger kids especially may get involved in what they're doing and forget who's around them. Make sure no drill groups are in an area that is in direct line of batted or thrown balls from another group. Volunteer coaches can provide invaluable supervision in practice and warm-ups during the game to help avoid accidents.

And since baseball is generally a warm-weather sport, encourage your players to bring water to practices and games and drink it regularly. Watch for indications of fatigue. Every child does not work at the same pace and level. At the younger levels, kids can fatigue quickly. Be sensitive to this, and when you see it, call for a water break or change to a less strenuous activity.

The Field

Foul lines are the lines drawn from the back tip of home plate extending in a straight line to poles in right field and left field. Fair territory is the playing field between the foul lines. Foul territory is the playing field outside the foul lines. The infield is the diamond-shaped playing area outlined by the bases, which are 60 feet apart in youth leagues. The outfield is the area beyond the infield to the outfield fences.

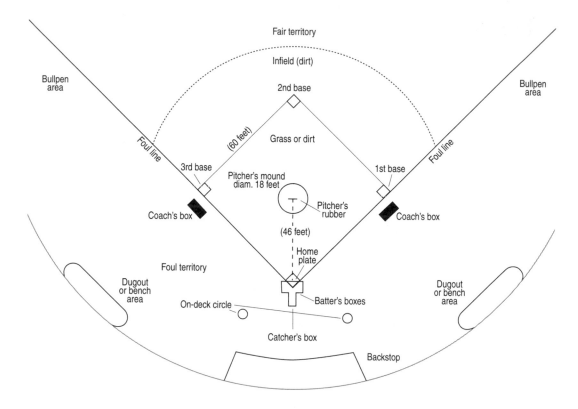

The *pitcher's mound* where the pitcher stands is at the center of the diamond. It can be a flat surface marked by a pitching plate or *rubber*, or it can be a raised mound. In youth leagues, it is 46 feet from home plate.

The *batter's boxes* are 4-foot-by-6-foot squares on either side of home plate, marking where the batter must stand when swinging at a pitch. The *catcher's box* is where the catcher is positioned prior to each pitch. The *coach's boxes* are two 4-foot-by-8-foot areas 6 feet back from first base and third base where coaches can communicate with their players on offense. The *on-deck circle* is for the next player at bat.

The *backstop* is the high fencing behind home plate. The *bench* or *dugout* is the area behind both base paths connecting to home plate where the coaches and players sit. The home team sits on the third base side of the diamond; the away team sits on the first base side. The *bullpens* are in foul territory way off the field of play, giving each team an area where substitute pitchers may warm up.

CHAPTER 3

DESIGNING YOUR PRACTICE

Mostly it's the smells that take you back. The smell of fresh-cut grass when you first walk out onto the field. The smell of baseballs and the smell of powdery resin.

—STEVE GARVEY

The games are what everyone looks forward to, but practice sets the tone for your team's entire experience. Conduct all your interactions with the players and other coaches with respect, enthusiasm, and a winning attitude, and you've gone a long way in setting the tone for your players' future success, in anything.

First make some notes or an outline about what your goals are for your players and your team. What do you want to achieve? Then, guided by this book and the suggestions in this chapter, make more notes about how to achieve your goals. Next, write a sample practice plan. Then tinker with it until you have a plan you're ready to start with. After your practices, make more notes. Evaluate how the different drills were handled by your team. What was too difficult? What are your team's weak areas? Strong areas? Jot down some ideas for the next practice and modify your practice plan accordingly. The more organized you are for practice, the more relaxed you'll be during practice, and the more fun you and your players will have.

Coaching, however, is not an exact science. It really is an art to bring together a group of young people and teach them to work as a team to accomplish goals. Every group will be a little different. What worked for last year's team is likely not going to be what this year's team needs. Be open and flexible. Your players are going to be learning a lot of new things about the sport, and you can learn a lot of new things about coaching too—no matter how many teams you've coached.

Before beginning each drill, clearly describe the drill and what is being emphasized. Explain any terminology and use it consistently so there is no breakdown in communication between you and your team. Keep your descriptions as short as possible. Keep the kids involved by asking them questions to see if they understood what you were talking about. Get them actively trying out the new skill or move as quickly as possible. Expect hustle, be positive, and keep the practice moving. Stay within the time allotted for each drill. For skills that need particular improvement, you can add activities and drills into the next practice plan. After the drill, you may choose to bring your players back together as a group and briefly go over the results, possibly having a player particularly adept at the skill demonstrate.

Insist that your players respect the game, their teammates, and their coaches. This can translate into simple acts: taking care of equipment (like not throwing the batting helmet); always being encouraging to teammates; and listening without fooling around when a coach is speaking.

Last, but certainly not least, have fun as you work on individual and team improvement!

Confident Coach's Drill Guide

The charts and practice plans that follow are designed to start you out with a basic model. As you get familiar with your drills and with your players, you will get more comfortable with using the drills most appropriate for your team and designing your own practice plan.

This book presumes that players in Group II will begin to pitch before the end of the season, so all the beginning pitching drills (which help all your players practice correct throwing technique) are included for this level. Catching drills are also included with the presumption that players will begin catching for these beginning pitchers. Bunting is an advanced but important skill included for Group III. However, if you have a young Group III team that hasn't played much baseball, you may decide you are not going to introduce bunting right away. These are guidelines. You're the coach, and ultimately, you will discern what's best for your team. Remember, baseball is a game. Your job as the coach is to enhance your players' enjoyment of the game.

PRACTICE PLAN GUIDE

Skills	Group I	Group II	Group III
Throwing/Catching (Chapter 4)	All drills All games	All drills All games	All drills Game 2
Hitting (Chapter 5)	Drills 1–5, 10 All games	All drills All games	All drills
Base running (Chapter 6)	Form drills 1–3 Baserunning drills 1–3 All games	All drills All games	All drills All games
Fielding (Chapter 7)	Drills 1–6 All games	Drills 2–10 All games	Drills 2–15
Pitcher (Chapter 8)	Drill 7 Limited bullpen All games	Drills 1–7 Bullpen All games	All drills Bullpen
Catcher (Chapter 9)	— All games	All drills All games	All drills
Bunting (Chapter 10)	—	—	All drills All games

Sample Practice Plans

Group I (1½ hours)

1:00 Practice overview

1:05 Jog

1:10 Throwing mechanics
       Knee drill
       Shoulder point drill
       Twist drill

1:20 Play catch with partner

1:25 Ground balls with coaches (2–3 lines)
       Fly balls with coaches (2–3 lines)

1:35 Baserunning
       Home to first
       Home to second

    1:45 Hitting stations
            High ball (backstop)
            Batting tee (backstop)
            Step drill (home plate/hit out to field)
    2:00 Situation drill
    2:10 Live scrimmage
    2:25 Review and conclude

Group II (1½ hours)

    1:00 Practice overview
    1:05 Jog/light stretch
    1:10 Throwing mechanics
            Knee drill
            Shoulder point drill
            Twist drill
    1:20 Play catch with partner
    1:25 Ground balls and throws with coaches (2–3 lines)
            Fly balls and throws with coaches (2–3 lines)
    1:40 Hitting stations
            High ball (backstop)
            Batting tee (backstop)
            Step drill (home plate/hit out to field)
    2:00 Live batting practice with fielding (3 groups)
            Group 1 — hitting
            Group 2 — fielding
            Group 3 — batting tee (backstop)
    2:20 Baserunning
    2:25 Group review and conclusion

POSSIBLE PRACTICE PLAN SUBSTITUTIONS:
Bunting — 10 minutes
Sliding — 5 minutes

Group III (1¾ hours)

    1:00 Practice overview
    1:05 Jog around field/light stretch

EXPERIENCE TALKS   Always tune in to your players to make sure they are working hard and not getting bored. Again, what is done in a drill will show up in the games! If they are bored, you may not be moving through the drill sequences quickly enough. You don't have to belabor a point; you can address it again at the next practice. Keep the players—and the drills—moving.

1:10   Throwing mechanics
       Knee drill
       Shoulder point drill
       Twist drill
1:20   Live catch and throw with crow hop
       Ground balls
       Fly balls
1:30   Team relays from home plate to center field
1:40   Infield ground balls (2 groups if possible)
       Outfield fly balls
       Catcher blocking drills
1:50   Water break
1:55   All team relays and backups for different situations
2:10   Soft toss stations/live fielding (3 groups)
       Group 1—tee (home plate/hit out to field/players
       make plays)
       Group 2—high ball (backstop)
       Group 3—step (other side of backstop or alternative location)
2:25   Live batting practice (3 groups)
       Group 1—in field
       Group 2—at bat (run last hit out)
       Group 3—batting tee work at backstop
2:40   Review and conclude

POSSIBLE PRACTICE PLAN SUBSTITUTIONS:
Baserunning — 10 minutes
Bunting offense and defense — 15 minutes
Sliding — 5 minutes
Team pop-up defense/communication — 10 minutes

PART II
ESSENTIAL SKILLS

CHAPTER 4

LEARNING THE BASICS: THROWING AND CATCHING

People ask me what I do in winter when there's no baseball. I'll tell you what I do. I stare out the window and wait for spring.

—ROGERS HORNSBY

A father and son playing catch conjures up images of a Norman Rockwell painting. Adults and children have bonded over this activity for generations in our country.

But when it comes to playing baseball, the reality is that the critical skills of throwing and catching correctly are not emphasized enough. Kids develop bad habits early, using incorrect techniques that cause poor performance and, in some cases, injury. Incorrect throwing form leads to inaccuracy, which leads to errors. This can be most discouraging. Trial and error with multiple repetitions represents the best formula for long-term success, a formula not used often enough. This means that as a coach, you give your young player the opportunity to fail while he's learning so he can start to feel for himself what feels right and works, and what doesn't feel right and doesn't work. Keep encouraging him and instructing him throughout the process.

The first part of every baseball practice should involve throwing and simple catching, followed by drills that increase the level of difficulty of both skills. Team defense starts with every teammate's ability to catch. On many plays, this means one teammate throwing the ball accurately to another teammate. For young players, this is a monumental task.

Breaking down the mechanics will allow for proper technique in throwing the baseball. *Perfect practice makes the skill permanent.* Teaching a youngster to throw the ball properly may be one of the most important aspects of coaching baseball.

How to Throw

Start with each player having a ball in hand to work on the grip. Obviously, the size of the players' hands will have an effect on this. Very young players may find it easier to start practicing a proper hold with a softer ball. Show the players the seams on the ball. Their goal should be to grab the ball across the largest seam with the middle and pointer finger doing the bulk of the work. The thumb should be underneath.

A common mistake is for players to *choke* the ball, or grab it too tightly. This tension will cause problems with accuracy and arm strength that are the opposite of what they are trying to accomplish. There should be just enough space between the ball and the palm to pass, say, a piece of cardboard through. No death grips on the ball!

Now, show the actual throwing motion. This exercise is simple but will force proper throwing technique if done enough in your practices. To start, have the player point his glove-hand shoulder at an imaginary teammate and with the ball in hand, palm up, proceed to circle his arm by barely brushing his leg as he extends his arm *down*, then continues the motion *back*, and then *up* with the ball.

Pointing the shoulder keeps the shoulder *closed*. If the shoulder is not pointing at the target and the chest is exposed, this is called *open*. Many throwing errors at every level are the result of *opening up*. This changes the angle of the arm and results in decreased accuracy and possible injury.

To review:

1. **Down:** The ball goes to the knee, forcing a full extension of the arm.

2. **Back:** Continue the arm circle back, arm slightly bent.

3. **Up:** Finish up, with the arm bent and the elbow at shoulder level. This is the ball release point.

Dummying this motion for a couple of minutes before your players start throwing, especially early in your season, will give your players a foundation for proper throwing mechanics. You can come back to this teaching tool until your players realize that these steps—down, back, up—are necessary to throw a baseball well.

Now, as your players get ready to release the ball, their eyes need to be focused on the target: the person they are throwing to. This is critical. At the point of release, each player wants the ball centered in his hand in a solid grip—but not in a squeeze, as that will affect accuracy.

After the motions of down, back, and up, the player releases the ball with a snap of the wrist. As the ball leaves his hand, his thumb is pointed down and his middle finger should be the last part of his hand to touch the ball. Multiple repetitions will be necessary before your players become good at this.

WATCH FOR . . . turning the wrist while releasing the ball. This will cause movement on the ball, which is the last thing the receiver wants. The slightest deviation from a proper release will result in the ball not going straight to the target, which is obviously the goal when fielders throw to each other. Let your players save the sliders, sinkers, and curves for the pitchers!

How to Catch

Catching a baseball seems like a simple act. But to a young player at the learning stages of his development, it can be a difficult experience. Fear of being hurt by the baseball can be learned at a very young age. It hurts when the pitcher's throw hits you, and it hurts when a ground ball takes a bad bounce and hits you. Major league players still fear being hit by a baseball.

This aspect of the game has to be dealt with by everyone who puts on a uniform.

Young players can practice with a softer baseball. These balls do not hurt as much and help ease the fears of young players—and their parents. Anything a coach can use to promote the confidence and performance of

the players is beneficial. As much as possible, anticipate their needs and, when you can, protect your players.

A player catching a ball must maintain a balanced and athletic position. This is when the player is on the balls of his feet and has them spread slightly wider than his shoulders. Knees are bent slightly to give a low center of gravity, giving him a solid base for quick athletic movement in all directions. This position allows players to maintain better balance as they catch the ball.

Make learning how to catch a fun exercise. You can explain to the players that catching a baseball is like catching an egg, then challenge them to catch the ball the way they would catch an egg. If a player *fights* the catch, that is, jabs her hand hard forward, then the egg is likely to shatter or be dropped. *Soft hands* is a positive affirmation for any baseball player. Simply stated, it means that the player is able to handle the ball without bobbling, dropping, or fighting the ball.

When catching, the hands are always ready. A quick ground ball or line drive must be handled in milliseconds. The glove should be open and fully exposed to prevent any delays from getting ready. Continually stress to the players the importance of using two hands whenever catching the

ball. This may not be physically possible to do on balls requiring a full extension, but most of the time a ball player can catch with two hands. The catch is finished by watching the ball into the glove, and then, upon impact, gently squeezing the glove hand and putting the other hand on top of the ball. Emphasizing the importance of actually keeping an eye on the ball until it is caught sounds so very basic, but it is the cause of many errors—even at the major league level. Don't allow your players to catch correctly some of the time and carelessly other times. Teach, correct, and review the importance of this fundamental: you are teaching muscle memory that will translate into success.

The position of the hands for balls hit above the waist, below the waist, to the glove side, and to the backhand side of the glove are positions you want to demonstrate and constantly review for your young players. Developing a common language allows you to communicate quickly and efficiently—which is the key to being an effective coach.

- **Thumb-to-thumb.** For balls received above the waist, use the term *thumb-to-thumb*. The thumb in the glove and the thumb of the throwing hand are in close proximity as the ball is being received, so the ball can be secured by the throwing hand as soon as it is in the glove. With the throwing hand near the ball, the receiver can then grab the ball out of her glove and throw it without any wasted motion.

- **Pinky-to-pinky.** For balls received below the waist, use the term *pinky-to-pinky*. Having two pinky fingers in close proximity requires the player to open the mitt down toward the ground and allows her to comfortably cushion any ball received. If the ball comes in below the waist, and the player tries to catch it thumb-to-thumb with her mitt up, she is much more likely to push the ball away rather than catch it.

- **Glove side.** For balls received away from the middle of the body on the glove side, use the term *glove side*. You want to encourage your players to move to receive the ball as close to the center of the body as possible, but players will not always be able to achieve this. If possible, the player uses two hands and the thumb-to-thumb approach. If the ball is coming in away from the middle of the body and below the waist, have your players bend their knees to receive it.

⚾ **Backhand.** For balls received in the area of the player's throwing hand, use the term *backhand*. Similar to tennis, the fielder is now going to reach across her body; as she does, she turns the glove over so that her thumb is facing the ground. Remind the player to keep her glove open. The throwing hand will stay in the thumb-to-thumb position for as long as physically possible to allow for a quick exchange from catching to proper grip to throwing. For any ball hit below the waist on a backhand, simply bend at the knees and maintain the glove in the backhand position.

WATCH FOR . . . a player reaching for the ball with his glove hand first, then bringing in his throwing hand — which was extended away from the glove — to secure the ball and get into throwing position. These moves need to happen simultaneously. A delayed technique results in dropped balls, wasted time if the ball needs to be thrown to a base or cutoff man, and an unbalanced position which results in an awkward athlete.

Drills

For these first four drills—the throwing set—have players partner up across from each other in two lines. Or spread the partners out on different areas of the field. Be sure they have room so an errant throw will not accidentally hit a teammate. Make these positions permanent, so at the start of practice there is no wasted time when you announce, "Throwing drills." Keep the drills moving and keep a watchful eye out for mechanical breakdown. Remember, whatever your players are doing in the drills, they will transfer into games. You are trying to teach muscle memory and you may be correcting players who have thrown incorrectly for years. Be alert and patient. You can expect to start seeing results after just a few practices.

The throwing drills are followed by catching drills. Then your team can progress to the drills in the fielding chapter, which practice both skills and begin to work on team defense.

1. KNEE

Start with partners facing each other, spaced 15 to 20 feet apart; for very young players, space them 10 to 15 feet apart. Have each player on his strong-side knee: the right knee for right-handed throwers, left knee for left-handed throwers. Now practice the mechanics described earlier in the chapter: *down, back, up.* Encourage the players to *scrape the ground* with the ball as they go down. This will force them into full arm extension and discourage *short-arming* the ball, a very prominent and poor mechanic found often in youngsters when they bring their arm too tight to their bodies. Point out, however, that the elbow should not be locked. Remind them to "Point your shoulder." They

should aim it at their partner just before releasing the ball to him. This improves accuracy immeasurably and creates the habit of throwing this way naturally. Younger players will be giddy at first, but once they realize the significance of the drill and what the results can be, they will get competitive. Success with this drill will not happen overnight, but your players will progress quickly once they master the proper throwing technique.

Walk through, or dummy, this drill to start. With the players on their knees, have them mimic the drill, ball in hand, without throwing. Coaches can walk around and verbally and physically correct the mechanics. Then you can do the drill live with balls from the same position. Balls will be

---

 EXPERIENCE TALKS At the conclusion of fundamental drills, bring your players in for review. Explain some positive things you saw, as well as what needs improvement. This is not a speech, but rather 15 to 20 seconds of key teaching points. If a pair has done the drill particularly well, have them demonstrate. This makes these players feel good and provides a peer model others can strive for. If weaker players show improvement, recognize them. Once you've made your points, have your players hustle back to their spot for the next drill. Always encourage your players to hustle. This sets a tone and makes practice move quickly. The one thing a player can control is his level of effort. Build on this for your team's development.

flying everywhere; what's important is you're providing your players with an opportunity for multiple repetition, proper correction, and constant encouragement.

DURATION: 1–4 minutes

2. SHOULDER POINT

This drill is a progression from the knee drill. Partners are standing for this drill about 15 to 20 feet apart, with their glove-side shoulders pointed at their partner. Their feet should be slightly wider than shoulder width, knees bent.

They are now going to play catch from this position, using the same down, back, up movement as they did in the knee drill. They cannot scrape the ground but will use the same motion. Keep reminding them of the importance of being balanced and bringing the throwing elbow at or above shoulder level. If the elbow drops, the angle of the ball leaving the hand changes dramatically and the thrower will have little chance of hitting his target.

DURATION: 1–4 minutes

WATCH FOR . . . throwers getting off balance; the elbow dropping too low; eyes not on the target.

3. TWIST

For this drill, your players will build on the movements of the first two drills by adding a twist. The change is the partners face each other squarely, 15 to 20 feet apart, in a balanced, athletic position. The upper-body twist is what points the glove-hand shoulder at the target. Feet stay stationary, forcing the twisting action. The player needs to turn his body to get the glove-side shoulder pointed to his target, then proceed into the *down, back, up* motion and release the ball with a snap of his wrist. Keep-

ing the shoulder as *closed* as possible—pointed in the direction of the throw during the throwing sequence—will prevent poor throwing motion. An open shoulder makes the proper down, back, up movement physically impossible. As the players throw back and forth in this drill, they will begin to experience the importance of balance essential to throwing.

DURATION: 1–4 minutes

4. CROW HOPPING AND PLAYING CATCH

This drill puts all of the steps of the former drills together to teach players how to play catch easier with the *crow hop*. When fielding a throw, ground ball, or pop-up, the player is basically in the position of the twist drill, his body square and facing where he needs to throw. The challenge of getting from this position to the throwing position with the shoulder pointed toward the target is accomplished by a crow hop. To crow hop, a player quickly shuffles or slides his feet so that the foot on the side of his throwing arm will be slightly in front of the other, the heel of the front foot even with the toe of the back. Again, the feet should be slightly wider than shoulder width, knees bent.

First, do this drill dry without balls. Gather the players to teach the concept and let them dummy it by first pretending to catch a ball. Then walk them through, getting them into throwing position by simultaneously shuffling their feet—to put their lower body in this crow hop position—and twisting, as in the previous drill. When you feel your players understand the movements well enough dry, try the drill with balls, making sure you continue to coach, correct, and encourage as they put all the moves together.

DURATION: 4–6 minutes

WATCH FOR... grandiose jumping instead of crow hopping. Explain they are not so much jumping into position as shuffling into position. You can demonstrate the difference and have them see how much precious time is lost if players add in a distinct jump. They may also want to do this whole sequence too fast; don't let them!

5. HAND AND GLOVE POSITIONS

A simple exercise when introducing catching skills is to gather the team together and review the different positions for the throwing hand and glove, described earlier in the chapter. Show each position, explain the importance of using two hands, and demonstrate the kind of errors that can happen if players aren't in proper position. Then shout out commands, using the four position options: thumb-to thumb, pinky-to-pinky, glove side, backhand. As your players start to get the calls, you can shout out the commands quicker and correct on the fly. Correcting one youngster in a positive way will benefit the entire group.

DURATION: 2–4 minutes

6. CATCHING GROUND BALLS

Partners are in two lines, 20 feet apart, facing each other. Instruct one line to throw five ground balls to their partners in the other line. These should be easy ground balls, allowing the other player the chance to work on catching and getting into throwing position. Most young players will break down during this drill. They will speed up mentally and their bodies

will follow in the rush, causing them to get off balance, drop their elbow too low, and lose sight of the target. Insist once again that they see the ball into their glove pinky-to-pinky, crow hop into their throwing position, get on balance, and execute the throwing technique that has just been worked on so extensively. Once the first line has thrown five grounders, the second line does the drill, throwing five grounders.

DURATION: 2–4 minutes

7. CATCHING POP-UPS

Partners are in two lines, 20 feet apart, facing each other. Have one line throw five pop-ups to their partners; partners then throw five pop-ups back. Make sure players are moving their feet and working to get into position to catch the ball in front of themselves—not over their heads where they cannot see it. Once the catch is made, it is followed by a crow hop into the practiced down, back, up throwing technique.

DURATION: 2–4 minutes

Games

1. PICKLE

This game can get a little wild in terms of practicing proper catching and throwing form, but if you need a game for your younger players to let off some steam, here it is. Divide your team into threesomes. For the Group I level, have two players stand 15 to 20 feet apart, each on some kind of base or square drawn in the dirt that can be tagged; the third person is a baserunner. For Group II, players can be farther apart, even using bases on the diamond to be 46 feet apart. The goal of the runner is to run from base to base, "scoring" as many times as possible. The goal of the basemen is to get this runner out. The baserunner starts by beginning the run from one base to the other. The fielders react to the position of the runner by throwing the ball back and forth in an attempt to tag the baserunner out. The baserunner changes direction as often as possible, and the basemen can run after him. Once the runner is tagged out, he becomes a baseman. The winner is the one who tags the most bases before being tagged out.

STEP IT UP: There are many regional variations to this game. You and your players might know some. In one variation, several baserunners run between the two basemen; the last two players tagged out become the basemen.

DURATION: 5–10 minutes

2. IN THE CAN

Put an empty trash barrel at home plate. Send the players out to short centerfield, each with a ball, or with a few balls they put down well behind them so no one will trip. The players take turns trying to throw the ball into the barrel. Adjust the distance for your age group.

DURATION: 5–10 minutes

CHAPTER 5

LEARNING THE BASICS: HITTING

More mistakes are made hitting than in any other part of the game.
—TED WILLIAMS

Hitting a baseball is often considered the most difficult skill in sports to accomplish. Not only is it difficult to contact a small moving ball with a bat, but the spotlight is on that youngster as everyone watches. This pressure can be intimidating and, if not handled well, has the potential to steer a kid away from baseball altogether.

Hopefully, this chapter will help you do just the opposite: teach your players how to achieve such success in the batter's box that they want to play baseball every time they get the chance. Teaching a youngster to hit a baseball can be one of the most rewarding events of your coaching experience. Your kids may have a slugger from their favorite professional team whom they idolize—and they're ready to practice to be just like him.

Challenges of Hitting

Understanding the challenges faced by kids learning to hit will make you a more effective coach and help you facilitate their success. Your players may be afraid of the ball, afraid of looking inept, afraid of their team's reaction or a parent's reaction, afraid of not measuring up, afraid of total failure. Your job as a coach is to help ease these fears in every way possible.

Doing hitting drills on a regular basis is not foolproof, but over time, this repetition will give even your most challenged hitter a framework for improvement. Having your players achieve even simple goals can build understanding and confidence—and confidence is vital to the success of anything in life, especially hitting.

EXPERIENCE TALKS

Maybe more than any other well-known sport, baseball has a language of its own. Be diligent about explaining and demonstrating the baseball terms you are going to use.

For example, when the Carroll family's son was playing baseball in third grade, his dad—a professional coach, but not for baseball—was helping coach the team. Because of the particular game situation, the two fathers coaching were telling the kids from time to time to "Take the pitch!" Watching from the sidelines, Mom thought this meant swing—and that's what the kids were doing. Since *take the pitch* actually means don't swing at the pitch but let it go by, the coaches were getting frustrated—assuming the kids were getting rattled every time and swinging by mistake. Deducing what might be going on, after the game Mom suggested asking their son what *take the pitch* meant to him. Their son verified that, indeed, he and his teammates thought when a coach called out, "Take the pitch," they were supposed to swing!

Building the Hitter

As a coach, you're not expected to be an expert on hitting—or any other area of baseball, for that matter. What you can bring to your team is a working understanding of simple concepts. Share what you know in clear terms and avoid giving out information you're not sure about. Talk a lot about hitting. Remind your players how much practice it takes to become a good hitter. Offer corrections with the intent of improving the hitter, not criticizing. Find the good in any given player's hitting technique and point it out.

You can also constructively prepare your players for the failure that goes along with learning to hit. Point out some of the leading hitters in baseball, noting that if a major league player fails to hit seven out of ten times, they are a star. Bringing these examples to young players can ease any pressure they feel about being perfect hitters.

Make sure your players know the rules of baseball. Teaching and reviewing the strike zone can help hitters at all levels. Home plate is 17 inches wide,

THE STRIKE ZONE

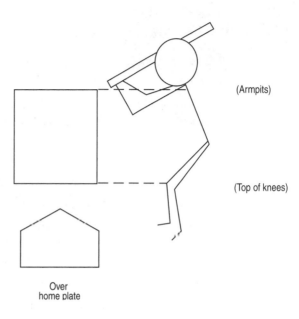

(Armpits)

(Top of knees)

Over home plate

but it can feel like 17 miles to a young hitter trying to connect with the ball. The area over home plate from the top of the letters on a uniform shirt to the top of the knees is how the rule book defines the strike zone. The more kids take in the concept of the strike zone and where it falls, the more they will be able to make the decision to only swing at strikes.

EXPERIENCE TALKS If you watch highlights of outstanding hitters on television, the hitter often appears not to be swinging very hard. Actually, what can be key in a powerful swing is that it is quick and fluid *and* conducted from a balanced position. This is not easy to do and requires that everything goes right, but anyone who has experienced this kind of hit knows what an awesome feeling it brings. In fact, hitting like this is so euphoric, it can become a craving!

Hitting Basics

Balance

Balance is critical for hitting, yet it is one of the most overlooked aspects of baseball skill, even in the major leagues. The pitcher is often trying to strike the hitter out by getting him off balance. In fact, hitters often strike themselves out by putting themselves in an unbalanced, awkward physical position that dramatically reduces their effectiveness. Young athletes find it particularly tough to maintain balance. Their physical coordination is still a work in progress. Teaching balance in a group setting lets kids see that everyone has something to learn; balance isn't necessarily innate. A batter in a strong, balanced stance can survive difficult pitches the same way a house built on a strong foundation can survive difficult weather. Kids can understand this analogy and build on this skill.

Gather your players around you and have them get into a batting stance with an imaginary bat in their hands. You will immediately see about 90 percent of them off balance; go around and give a slight push to their shoulders and send them flying. Review the balance stance: feet slightly wider than their shoulders, ankles and knees flexed comfortably, weight on the balls of their feet. Many young players start with their weight on their heels, so help them adjust their weight forward. Now have them all pick up their bat and get into their stances. Give a slight push again as you walk around. Congratulate them on their important improvement and emphasize that this is the way to prepare to hit.

Grip

In the beginning, don't dwell on grip. With the combination of nervousness, fear, and competitiveness that a young hitter brings to the plate, the bat can become the release point for these emotions. Any tension in the hands and swing destroys the rhythm necessary to succeed, so helping the hitter physically relax is invaluable. Keep your instructions simple with easy tips he can use, even when he's up at bat and under the spotlight. As your players begin to get the feel of the basic mechanics, you can come back and focus on the importance of the grip.

Right-handers will have their right hand on top and their left hand below when they hold the bat; left-handers will reverse this. The most common mistake is gripping the bat too tightly. The bat needs to be held

firmly, not tightly: no stranglehols. To
help your players relax, tell them to *play
the piano*. This means moving the fingers
while the bat is in launch position. This
forces them to keep their hands relaxed
and not bring unnecessary tension into
the grip.

Have your players practice a good
grip by holding the barrel of the bat, then
extending it parallel to the ground in front
of their waist, then gently raising the barrel slightly. Have them maintain
this grip as they move the bat into the launch position from where they
would start their swing.

Launch

The launch position is simply where the bat is prior to the start of the
swing. Each hitter will have a slightly different launch position, and
this is okay. The bat is held upright, above the back shoulder but not
touching it. For right-handers, the bat will be over the right shoulder; for
left-handers, the bat will be over the left shoulder. This position forces
the front shoulder to be closed, which is critical. As the ball comes in,
the hitter takes a stride and the hands bring the bat back and up. This is
called *cocking* the bat.

Stride

The stride is the step the hitter takes as the pitched ball
is coming toward him. This generally causes immediate
balance issues for young players. The stride should be
4 to 6 inches, with the front foot landing parallel to
the pitching rubber. The head stays down and the front
shoulder stays closed.

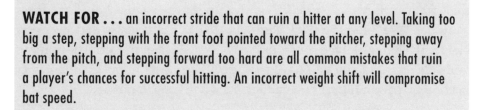

WATCH FOR . . . an incorrect stride that can ruin a hitter at any level. Taking too
big a step, stepping with the front foot pointed toward the pitcher, stepping away
from the pitch, and stepping forward too hard are all common mistakes that ruin
a player's chances for successful hitting. An incorrect weight shift will compromise
bat speed.

Swing

Ask your young players how they can create the bat speed they all want to create, and you will hear answers that involve just about every part of the body, except the body part most responsible for speed: the hands. If the hands are properly gripping the bat (when the swing goes from launch position to contact), the palm of the top hand is angled slightly downward. When the swing is done properly, the batter will have a sense of swinging down; but once contact is made, the swing flattens out, enabling the player to hit the center of the ball with the fat part, or barrel, of the bat. The batter continues with a follow-through, finishing with his hands high to maximize bat speed.

Starting from launch position, slowly demonstrate how a hitter wants to connect his bat with the ball over the middle of home plate. The batter keeps his head down and his front shoulder closed. The swing sends the bat to the ball without any wasted motion. If the bat travels in a semicircle, or the hitter steps away, this makes the swing longer and inefficient. Being out of position in any way can start a whole range of problems. For instance, if the player pulls his head back, this shifts the weight to his heels; to compensate, he may loop his swing, getting to the ball in a round-about way that often exposes the lower half of the bat, which does not hit as hard.

Instill in your hitters that they must see the ball from the time it leaves the pitcher's hand until it makes contact with the bat or the catcher's mitt; they want to *stay on the ball*, not give up on the swing. Label the front shoulder "Ike" and the back shoulder "Mike" and insist that on every swing, the hitter's chin goes from Ike to Mike. Teach this critical point to your players, and you will have provided them with an invaluable key to becoming a good hitter: you cannot hit what you cannot see.

EXPERIENCE TALKS "Every major league baseball team has a hitting coach overseeing just this aspect of the game," says Coach Kevin O'Brien. "Even though hitters at this level are the best in the world, and phenomenally skilled athletes, the slightest loss of timing, technique, or confidence can mean a prolonged slump. When teaching this skill, gather your players and review the fundamentals often. The review not only serves as a self-check for the players, but over time will increase their knowledge and understanding of hitting."

Drills

Safety is paramount whenever hitting is taking place. A thrown or hit ball, a thrown bat, or a bat being swung can all cause serious injury. Coaches must set hitting drills up in a very organized and supervised manner. Use any assistant coaches you have, or any parents who may be watching. Supervision allows your players to get in more hitting practice in a safe environment. Be aware of fences that could send balls ricocheting.

Hitters must wear helmets. Drill into your players that after they hit in a game, or in a game simulation in practice, they must drop the bat, not throw it, as they begin their sprint to first base. Penalize any player who disregards either of these rules by taking away at bats. They will get the point as everyone loves to hit!

These drills start with the basic movements and progress to game-type situations. Drills 5 through 9 are soft toss drills where the hitter hits into the fence. Notice that the hitter is 8 to 10 feet away from the fence, not 4 or 5 feet like you may have seen at neighborhood diamonds. The reason you want this distance from the fence is so the coach can toss from a 45-degree angle on the open side of the hitter's body to get the ideal delivery on the toss. You are basically pitching to the hitter, but moving off to the side so you don't get hit. You can use baseballs, but you can also use tennis balls, Wiffle balls, or even knotted rags. Drill 11 sets up drill stations, so if you have enough coaches and/or parents, you can have three or four of these stations running and use your practice time more efficiently. If you are coaching alone and cannot have your players working on different skills simultaneously, the drills to focus on are high ball, spread, and step.

WATCH FOR . . . your batters having too tight a grip, a body off balance, an incorrect stride, or a head coming up and not following the ball. Your goal as a hitting instructor is to get your hitters to be able to make solid contact every time they're up. Building self-esteem is a constant part of teaching hitting. It is a process!

1. STRIDE

Have your players, with their bats, spread out and get in their stance. Review by calling out, "Feet wider than your shoulders; bend at your ankles and knees with the weight on the balls of your feet." Have them imagine a pole going through their bodies that will not allow them to lunge forward. Next have them step like they are about to hit the ball. A simple way to explain this is to tell them they are stepping on an egg and if they step too hard it will break. This will give them the sense of a soft landing; this is achieved by keeping 50 to 60 percent of their weight over the back foot. As they step forward, they cock the bat backward into the launch position. Now have them do this ten times on their own.

DURATION: 3–5 minutes

2. LAUNCH

The purpose of this drill is to teach balance while preparing to hit. Have the group get in a balanced position. Review the stride move in slow motion. Now talk about the hands. Remind players that the hands create bat speed, then have the hitters move the bat into launch position. Have the group go through this sequence ten times on their own. Some coaches call this *stride and glide*.

DURATION: 3–5 minutes

3. SLOW-MOTION HITTING

This drill follows the hitting sequence in slow motion and can be used both as an introduction and a review. Start by telling your players to get in a balanced position. Quickly observe if any player has too much weight on his heels, or the feet are too close or too open, and then make corrections. Next, work on the approach to the ball. On the *step* command, each player takes a stride as if moving toward the pitcher, foot parallel to the pitching rubber, while cocking his bat back to the launch position. Next, players start their swing. Correct any looping motions that are making swings unnecessarily longer.

STEP IT UP: Expand this drill by teaching kids how to react to different pitches, such as high or low, in or out. You can start in slow motion, and then speed it up. If the pitch arrives up and in, the player wants to turn his shoulder in to ensure it stays closed for protection and for the best swing. If the ball is low and away, the player wants to bend at the waist, almost getting level with the ball to visually follow the ball into the catcher's mitt.

DURATION: 3–5 minutes

4. SLAP

This drill reinforces all the mechanics of hitting and builds confidence. To start, players take their stance without their bats. They place the hand that grips the bat handle closest to the bottom in an open palm position in front of the waist. The other hand is raised, open palm, back to where the hitter "launches" her swing. Have the hitter bring the raised hand down to the hand at the waist in a slapping motion. When the hands connect, the hitter's head is down (*Ike* and *Mike*), watching the hands meet in simulation of the bat hitting

the ball. As this occurs, you can tell your players, "Squish that bug with your back foot." This forces the back foot to turn the hips into the ball. Players follow through by finishing with both their hands above the front shoulder and the head down. The weight transfer should take the hitter toward or across home plate.

Once your players understand the movements, have them do the sequence ten times on their own while you observe and correct. Remind them this is not a race. (And keep them focused on slapping to perform the drill, not to amuse each other!)

DURATION: 2–4 minutes

5. SOFT TOSS

Soft toss is a way to get in multiple swings in a short period of time and build muscle memory with consecutive repetitions. To set up, have the hitters face a fence or backstop, about 8 to 10 feet away, in ready position. The tosser is a coach or parent on one knee who tosses the ball from a 45-degree angle underhand into the strike zone of the hitter. Don't rush

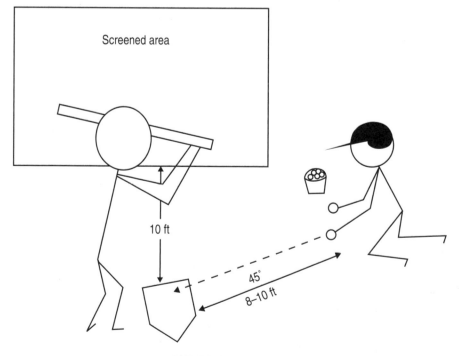

Screened area

10 ft

45°

8–10 ft

SOFT TOSS HITTING DRILL SETUP

the hitter; allow him to reset himself between pitches. Give each hitter five to eight swings.

STEP IT UP: Soft toss can also be done at home plate with fielders in their positions. This gives the hitter a chance to see where his hit balls are going, and gives the fielders a chance to make plays off the bat. Depending on your facilities and staffing, you could break your team into groups and do this drill with hitters and fielders at two or three locations and have everyone hit in half or one-third of the time.

DURATION: 10–15 minutes

6. HIGH BALL

This drill builds the swing of any hitter. Set up the same as you did in the soft toss drill. In this drill, the coach tosses the ball above and in front of the hitter's lead shoulder. This forces the hitter to get his bat (or club head) to the ball quickly. Any looping of the bat in this drill is exposed, because it results in missed or partially contacted balls. This drill is not designed to teach hitters to swing at balls out of their strike zone, but to force hitters to practice getting their hands *above the ball*. The reason for this is the hitter always wants the swing to go slightly down. If the bat goes underneath the ball, it's going to result in a pop-up, or a miss. But if the hitter keeps his hand above the ball and comes slightly down on the swing, it's likely to be a hard line drive. Give each hitter five to eight swings.

DURATION: 10–15 minutes

7. SPREAD

This drill takes away the stride step to focus on the role of the hands in creating bat speed. The basic setup is the same as the soft toss drill, only this time have the hitter take a balanced stance with his feet farther apart than usual. Proper use of the hands will produce a feel of the ball jumping off of the bat. The tosser is at a 45-degree angle and tosses the ball underhand toward the front hip of the hitter. This toss needs to be precise; if the hitter has to reach, the purpose of the drill is defeated. Have each player take five to eight swings, and then do a second round of the same thing if time permits.

STEP IT UP: Do this live with balls from home plate with fielders.

DURATION: 10–15 minutes

 EXPERIENCE TALKS Most major leaguers incorporate a spread drill into their pregame batting practice ritual. All-stars such as Albert Pujols and Tony Gwynn actually hit this way to eliminate any chance of getting off balance.

8. LOW BALL

Learning the strike zone is critical to becoming a great hitter. This drill teaches this while emphasizing the importance of keeping the head down. The setup is the same as the soft toss drill. The tosser, however, flattens out his angle and is in line with the hitter, about 8 to 10 feet away. The low ball toss is at the mid-thigh area. (Pitchers are taught to deliver the ball down, because balls up are more likely to produce hits and, at the higher levels, home runs.) Hitting this low ball will be impossible if any of the hands, balance, and approach techniques are violated; the player must be balanced with his head on the ball and his front shoulder going down and in, allowing his hands to get the bat to the ball quickly. In the initial stages, expect the hitters to swing and miss, usually because their heads are not following the ball. Give each hitter five to eight swings.

STEP IT UP: As the hitter improves at this drill, to help him practice the motion of hitting balls coming in low, toss the ball lower, below the player's knees. This drill can also be done from home plate. To make it more realistic, have players in the field making plays off the bat. On the last swing, have the hitter run the ball out.

DURATION: 10–15 minutes

 EXPERIENCE TALKS Oakland A's general manager Billy Beane finds highly disciplined hitters who understand and work the strike zone far more effective and valuable than those who do not have a good feel for the strike zone. The foundation for this understanding begins in youth baseball.

9. STEP

This drill teaches the hitter to maintain balance as she strides toward the pitch. The setup is the same as soft toss. The coach tosses the ball at a 45-degree angle at the middle of the plate, belt high. The tosser's goal is to make the toss easy to hit. During this drill, the tosser verbally commands "step" when the hitter needs to stride, as if at home plate in a game at bat. Watch for the front foot to land parallel to the pitching rubber and not open. Remind the hitter not to break the egg. Upon stepping, the hitter cocks her bat back to launch position and swings as she would in a game. Give each hitter five to eight swings.

DURATION: 10–15 minutes

10. BATTING TEE

Batting tee practice is a must for any baseball team, youth through majors. The tee allows the hitter to concentrate on hitting a stationary ball. Having a habit of seeing the ball will make all the difference when the hitter is actually swinging at a pitch. The tee also allows the player to take numerous swings without any fear of missing! Simply have the hitter take her stance and swing at the ball, attempting once again to incorporate the hands, balance, and approach method.

DURATION: 10–15 minutes

 EXPERIENCE TALKS Young kids have limited attention. Remote controls on their televisions and quick-response buttons on their video games and computers give them immediate choices. Baseball is by nature very methodical and does not operate in the same time frame as these modern-day advances. There is no instant success, which can be difficult for kids learning the game. If you have the personnel, run hitting stations as part of your practice to invigorate your players.

11. HITTING STATIONS

Divide your players into equal groups and have each group go to a hitting station with a different focus.

Station I	Batting tee	Station III	Step drill
Station II	High ball drill	Station IV	Live hitting/fielder

Assign a station to each smaller group (you can label them with their favorite pro team name) and then number each player. Tell the groups the next station they are to go to following the completion of their current station. Each player gets six swings per station. Coaches or parents time each station and yell, "Change!"—or get a whistle or air horn to signify the change. These stations can be adjusted to meet your needs. Use fewer stations if you have a limited number of players or staff.

DURATION: 15–20 minutes

Games

1. MOST LINE DRIVES

This game is set up like the spread drill, only it's done with balls at home plate. Each player gets a set number of tosses, say six to eight. The team can field for the player at bat, and coaches can keep score of who gets the most hits.

DURATION: 15 minutes

CHAPTER 6

LEARNING THE BASICS: BASERUNNING

Baseball is the only sport I know that when you're on offense, the other team controls the ball.

— KEN HARRELSON

In baseball, good baserunning can result in beating out an infield hit, stealing a base, or scoring on a ball in the gap. Bad baserunning can cost a team outs, scoring opportunities, and victories. Baserunning changes the whole tempo of a baseball game in a positive or negative way. You can make all your players better baserunners by teaching and drilling proper running form and baserunning technique.

Running Form

Speed is often an innate talent that allows some players to be great base stealers. But any player can become faster by becoming more efficient. Many athletes, even at the highest levels, run incorrectly. Most young players certainly do. They fight themselves by tensing up their bodies—hands, arms, and mouths. These runners may look like they are really putting out a maximum effort, but they are really defeating their goal of being the fastest runner they can be.

Form Drills

A few simple drills at the start of practice will instill habits that promote good running form. When you watch a track meet on television, you see some of the most fluid and efficient athletes in the world. There is no wasted motion when they run. Improving running form will take time, but you will be amazed at the results you will see from these drills in just a few weeks.

1. UPPER BODY

Have your players line up along either outfield foul line to begin. Share with them that tension is counterproductive to being a good runner and athlete. Tension causes the muscles to tighten up, which restricts range of motion and slows a runner down.

Now tell the players to imagine they are holding an egg in each hand with their palms up. If they squeeze too tight, the eggs will break. Next explain that as their arms brush against the sides of the rib cage, they should keep their arms moving as if they were reaching for a rope out in front. This will get your players leaning forward and using their arms as an asset. Eyes should be focused on the destination: the base. The jaw should be loose, not clenched.

Once they get the motion, have them practice this, basically in place, for 15 seconds. They will probably be silly at first, but as you build this into your practice warm-up, they will begin to take it more seriously.

DURATION: 1–2 minutes

2. DRUM MAJOR

The goal of this drill is to maximize the use of the legs. In the track world, this drill is called *high knees*; players want to try to get their knees high, even with their waist and parallel to the ground. This will let your players tap into a new force in their legs they didn't know they had.

Divide the team into four lines, three or four players per line. Have a coach about 20 yards away, or use a cone. Have them practice this high knees movement on their own. Then, with your players putting together this high knees movement and the arm movement from the previous drill, have each line go up to the coach and back. When the first line is about a quarter of the way to the coach, the second line can go, and then the next and the next. Have each line go up and back two times. Remind your players throughout the drill that this is not a race, but a chance to concentrate on their form.

DURATION: 2–4 minutes

3. LOWER BODY

This drill can also be called the trotting horse; in track circles, it's often referred to as butt kicks. The goal is to lengthen a player's stride. If a player's stride is 3 feet and you can increase it even slightly, think about the difference this will make just running to first. The player could pick up anywhere from a half step to a step and a half. To do this drill, the player kicks his heel to his rear, then brings that knee up so his thigh is parallel to the ground, then kicks his leg out for a long extension. He then repeats the movement with the other leg so he's basically doing exaggerated running. As

in the drum major drill, the lines go up to the coach and back twice, putting the movements from all three running form drills together, but concentrating on form, not speed.

DURATION: 2–4 minutes

4. FORM RUNNING

This drill puts everything together to "run" with this new form. The setup is the same as the previous drill. Have the first line go half speed to the coach, trying

to incorporate the movements in more of a run. Then the second group follows, and the third and the fourth. Let them do this once up and back. The second time up and back, have them increase the speed to about three-quarters of their full speed; they should still not be racing each other.

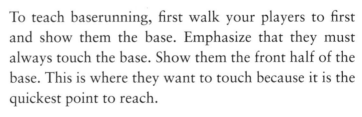

STEP IT UP: Once your players know this drill, it is a great way to warm up for practice, always at three-quarter speed, never at full speed.

DURATION: 5–7 minutes

Baserunning Mechanics

Running speed is a great attribute in a baseball player, but it's not the most important one. What's more important physically for running bases is that the player can accelerate to reach his top speed in as few steps as possible, can change direction, and can stop under control. In addition, the runner has to understand when to run.

Touch the Front Half of the Base

To teach baserunning, first walk your players to first and show them the base. Emphasize that they must always touch the base. Show them the front half of the base. This is where they want to touch because it is the quickest point to reach.

Watch the Foot and the Ball

Now demonstrate the proper body position for the run. As the runner touches the base, he wants to lower his head and watch the foot hit the base. Then, as he runs over the bag, he looks over his right shoulder to see if the ball has been overthrown. He can turn to look over his left shoulder, but if the umpire judges this turn as a move to advance to the next base, and the first baseman tags him, he's out. Coach your players to create this habit of looking over the right shoulder and their moves will not be open to interpretation by the umpire.

Run Through the Base

Next, teach them that on first, they want to run *through the base*. This means not slowing down as they touch the base because that could be just the amount of time the baseman needs to get the ball and tag the runner out. They want to run hard into the outfield an extra three or four full running steps beyond the base.

Round the Bag

Next, teach them on a ball hit to the outfield how to *round the bag*. This simply means as they are running down to first, about three-quarters of the way to the base, they move to run slightly outside of the baseline to give themselves a good angle for going to second if the ball is missed or bobbled by the outfielder (see diagram). As your runners get more accomplished, you can help them minimize this arc as they round the

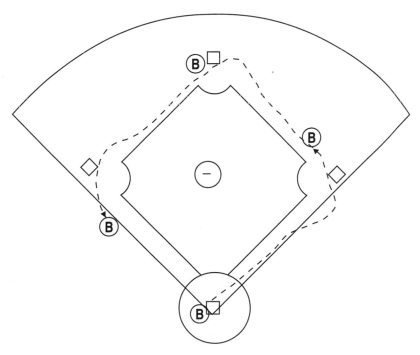

bag so as not to slow themselves down needlessly. At no point should the runner be more than about 6 feet outside the baseline, and most of the time, he will be much closer than that.

Baserunning Concepts

Now your players are ready to learn about running in game situations. Here are some simple guidelines.

The first critical rule is that once the hitter makes contact with the pitched ball, unless the ball is clearly foul, he immediately runs as hard as he can to first base, even if he thinks the ball will bounce or roll foul. Impress upon your players that running hard puts pressure on the defense to make the play, which could cause the fielders to bobble or miss the ball.

On all balls hit beyond the infield, the baserunner will assume he has the opportunity to reach second base. The quick turn at first base toward second base is done at top speed with a strong lean to the left. Runners overrunning second or third base can be tagged out immediately if they are not on base.

Once the other team has the ball back to the pitcher, the play is finished and the runner needs to stay on base. The runner cannot leave the base until the pitched ball has crossed over home plate and he cannot advance safely unless the hit ball is on the ground or in the air beyond the reach of the defensive players.

However, on two outs, all baserunners move on contact of the bat with the ball. With less than two outs, on fly balls hit to the outfield, although the runner may now be several steps toward the next base, she watches the outfielder make or miss a catch as she returns some steps toward the base. If the ball is caught, she sprints back to base. If, as she returns to base, the fielders get hold of the ball and are throwing it to her base, she slides to the base.

Sliding

A player slides in to the base to stop momentum at the base without stopping his speed. He can also use it to avoid a tag by sliding into the base away from the baseman who has the ball. In a slide, one leg is extended out to touch the base, one leg is bent back under the knee; the hands fly up and back into the air and the player leans back and down into the slide. Make sure your players learn to give themselves ample space, starting about three or four strides away, to complete the slide so they do not jam into the base. If the base is not a breakaway base, jamming into the base can result in injuries.

Diving

Diving to a base serves the same purpose as sliding. A player might dive when he is advancing to a base or has to return to a base. You can decide whether you want to practice diving for the base with your players or not. Players can hurt their fingers doing this, and most of them who want to dive for a base figure it out themselves. To dive, on the player's last stride he is already on his way down, so his center of gravity is low. He lands on his chest with his head up, his arms extended out to touch the base.

Stealing Bases

From T-ball through Little League, *leading*—moving off the base to get a head start to the next base—is not permitted. Stealing a base is permitted, however, after the ball has crossed home plate. This offers fast, aggressive players an opportunity to really help their team; and for some players, stealing becomes their favorite part of the game.

To *steal,* the runner starts toward the next base with his shoulders toward second and his knees bent, using the bag to push off. The more explosive the take-off a runner can achieve, the better success he'll have getting to the next base without getting thrown out. You can encourage your faster runners to "read" balls that are in the dirt to decide if they have enough advantage to run for the next base. Catchers are taught to block the ball, which means they stop it, retrieve it, and then throw it. This can give a runner time to get a good jump on the defense.

A *delayed steal* is valuable in trying to get the catcher off guard. Just as the catcher is about to release the ball to the pitcher, the runner takes off. This can result in the catcher *double clutching*, which means he starts to throw, pulls back, then goes to throw again, which can cause him to lose control of the ball as well as cause the basemen to be out of position. Consequently, the baseman could be forced to try to catch the ball on the move, which is much more difficult.

A *double steal* is another valuable technique. With men on first and third, the runner on first steals second. As the throw from the catcher goes over the pitcher's head toward second, the runner on third takes off for home. Remember, once the ball crosses the plate, the runners can steal. Watch out for an experienced catcher who will fake to second and throw to third.

WATCH FOR . . . your players slowing down before crossing the base, not rounding the bag, bringing their head up and not watching foot contact with the base, or stepping on the far half of the base — all improper techniques that could result in an out.

Baserunning Drills

These drills offer some different options for teaching and practicing baserunning. Use your time wisely; don't waste valuable practice minutes doing any running drill that is not relative to your players' abilities and needs.

1. BASERUNNING FORM

Have your team line up halfway down the first baseline. At your direction, the first player runs full speed, using good form running, touching the home plate side of the base with her head down, turning to look over her right shoulder, and running through the base. As the first player nears first base, the second player can run, until everyone has had a turn. Have a token penalty for missing any of these points, like five pushups. Your team will like this challenge and it will make them concentrate on these important fundamentals.

STEP IT UP: The runners can start from home plate. You can also incorporate the slap drill from the hitting chapter to have them practice good jumps out of the box.

DURATION: 2–4 minutes

2. ROUNDING THE BAG

Have your players lined up at home plate with a cone on the baseline three-quarters of the way to first where they need to cut out to round to the base. As in the first drill, have the players, one at a time, run to first making sure they go around the cone, bob their head, and watch their foot touch the corner of first base. On the first round, have them turn hard and get back to the bag. On the second round, have them hesitate, imagine the outfielder bobbles the ball, and go on to second.

STEP IT UP: This setup can be done going from first to third or second to home or even first to home. You can also split your team and have half at home plate and half on second. The first hitter up simulates a hit by slapping his hands as before, then runs to second base. The runner at second base also reacts to the slap by running from second base to home. You can do different aspects of these depending on your level and the stage of the season.

DURATION: 3–5 minutes

3. HOME RUN

For this drill, all the players line up at home plate. Player number one initiates the simulated swing by slapping his front hand with his back hand, then immediately sprints toward first base on an inside-the-park home run. As the first hitter gets halfway to first base, the second hitter takes off. Runners want to be in a lean-in position toward the pitcher's mound, and in strong running form. This can be a great way to end your practice: everyone gets a home run!

STEP IT UP: For more advanced players, if everyone doesn't run this drill as hard as they can, you can have them do the drill again, calling out: "You can't hide in this drill; everyone can see you! Do it again!"

DURATION: 3–5 minutes

4. SLIDING

First, players take their shoes off and sit in a grassy area with both legs extended. Have them bend one leg and tuck it under the opposite thigh, then try this same position with the other leg to see which feels more comfortable. Next, players sit with their preferred leg tucked underneath and throw their arms and hands up and back. This raises both their legs and simulates the body action when a player enters the slide. Repeat this several times. Now have the players move about three to four strides from the base they will be sliding into, using their gloves for the base. Taking slow, easy strides; each player slides into base. As the players get comfortable with the slide, extend the distance from base and increase the speed. Let the players proceed according to their comfort level. If a player is uncomfortable, have him stop and start from the beginning again. The next step is to have players put their shoes on and line up starting on the base path about halfway between first and second base. One at a time, have the players sprint toward second and slide into the base.

STEP IT UP: As their confidence grows, players can begin sliding to the right of the base to tag the base with their left hand away from the defender's tag.

DURATION: 3–8 minutes

WATCH FOR . . . hands coming down during the slide or starting the slide too close to the base; both can result in injuries. The hands are reaching overhead, not ever coming in contact with the ground during the slide. Younger players may attempt to lessen the impact of hitting the ground by bracing with their hands. This can result in injury to the wrist and hands. Foot and ankle injuries are usually the result of starting the slide too close and jamming the foot against the base. Throwing the hands overhead also helps elevate the lead foot off the ground, preventing spikes from catching.

5. BASERUNNING SCENARIOS

This drill gives your players the experience of linking proper baserunning with game situations. To set up, have your players form a single line near home plate. If you can, have coaches standing in the coach's boxes at first and third, as you would in a game, instructing your players while the drill runs. Once the player completes his run, his turn is over and he jogs back to home plate in foul territory.

The first part of the drill teaches baserunners how to approach first base.

1. **Base on Balls** (pitcher has pitched four balls; runner is walking to first): Have all your players take a turn sprinting to first base. Teach them that this sets the atmosphere for the inning: "Here we come; we're going to have a big inning."

2. **Don't Rub It** (hit by a pitch): Have all your players once again take a turn sprinting to first base. The idea here is that they don't stand at home plate rubbing their elbow or whatever got hit.

3. **Infield Hit** (ball hit between the infielders, forcing the infielders to move some distance to get the ball and make an accurate throw across the diamond for an out): On this play and those to follow, the hitter can simulate a hit by establishing her batting stance, placing her left hand in front of her body at waist level, her right hand above her shoulder, then bringing her right hand down through the strike zone to slap her left hand for the "hit." Have your players take turns hitting and making an all-out sprint to first base; the faster they run, the harder it will be for the infielders to make a successful play.

4. **Outfield Hit** (but ultimately no opportunity to advance): Each player "hits," then rounds first base about a third of the distance to second base, then hustles back to first.

5. **Outfield Hit** (opportunity to advance): Each player "hits," makes the same turn as above, has the advantage because outfielders mishandled the ball, and continues sprinting to second base.

6. **Outfield Hit** (hitter has definite double, possible triple): Each player "hits," then takes a base run to second base into several steps to third, reads that he does not have the advantage to continue to third, and hustles back to second.

7. **Outfield Hit** (hitter has a definite triple and a possible home run): When approaching third base, the baserunner looks at the third base coach for direction. To signal the runner to continue, the coach circles his right arm in a clockwise direction. To signal the runner to slide to avoid a tag out, the coach is on one knee with

hands forward, palms down. To signal the runner to stop, no slide necessary, the coach stands with both arms extended above his head. To run this drill, have each player hit, then run the bases round toward third and respond to the direction of the coach.

DURATION: 10 minutes

Games

1. BURST

Create two parallel lines 10 to 15 feet apart. Have your team line up on one of the lines and then at your signal, accelerate with a burst of speed to cross the other line as quickly as possible. Do it a few times for warm-ups. The next run, have half the team (the kids who came in last) sit down. The kids left now run again, with the kids who came in last sitting down again, so you have two players competing against each other to see who can show the fastest acceleration that day. (Your players can also practice at home by creating a circle and standing in the center, bursting in all directions as fast as they can to cross out of the circle.)

DURATION: 5–7 minutes

CHAPTER 7

LEARNING THE BASICS: FIELDING

Good defense in baseball is like good umpiring. It's there, you expect it, but you don't really appreciate it. But when it isn't there, you notice it.

—DOUG DeCINCES

Defense in baseball is critical to the success of every championship team. While we live in an age where offense sells and fans crave the home run, good pitching surrounded by good defense will win every time.

Getting young players to become good defenders is a process for the coach, but continue repetition of the basics in your practice and you will see results. Baseball players with the ability to consistently field and throw the ball with accuracy will be successful. Fielding is essentially throwing and catching with a purpose; that purpose is to prevent baserunners from scoring.

Before the ball goes into play, good defensive players are always in a ready position with the glove hand and throwing hand open to receive the ball. This may not seem like a difficult skill in any given moment, but it is a difficult skill for young people to sustain in every inning of the game. Getting young players to stay alert is a challenge. In addition, you are often still working with the fear factor; kids may think they want to catch that ball, but when it zings in at them, they may not be so ready to get under it or behind it.

There are no easy remedies to these deterrents to playing successful baseball. The plain fact is with Group I and Group II teams, you will be coaching kids who will never play baseball again—because they didn't like the sport, because they didn't feel like they were any good, because it was their parents who wanted them to play in the first place.

Baseball is a great game for kids, so give all your players the opportunity to experience all the fielding positions in practice. But when it comes to game time, think about putting your more adept players in the infield. The kids who are staring at the clouds, watching butterflies, or kneeling to play in the dirt between batters will not be safe in the infield. And the parents who are upset by outfield assignments would likely be more upset if their son or daughter got hurt in your practice. Safety is paramount.

Over time, the kids who don't really want to play baseball are sifted out. By Little League level, the majority of the kids playing are ready to be baseball players—and ready to field that baseball. Once they've caught that fly ball for that big out, they'll be hooked.

The Positions

The pitcher and catcher are the only fixed positions, and then only at the beginning of the play. The other players move as needed to defend and prevent scoring a run. Players on their own, or at a coach's direction, can vary their locations depending upon game situations, such as number of outs, the count on the batter, and the number of runners on base.

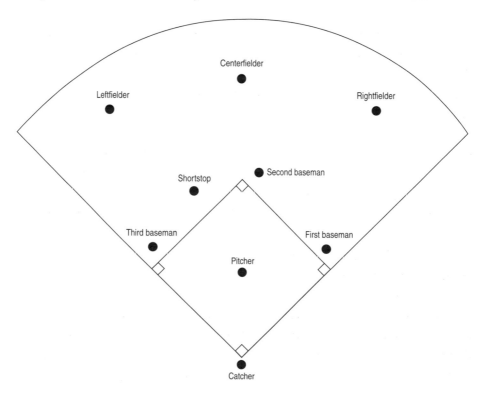

First baseman: This player needs to be adept at handling ground balls and incoming throws that may be off target. Agility is important, and height is a plus for handling high throws.

Second baseman: This player has a similar role to the shortstop in fielding a variety of hits, responding to baserunners, and following the game to understand the play needed. This position completes double plays by throwing to first and also backs up first base. Arm strength is not as critical for this position, but the ability to catch and throw accurately is.

Shortstop: This player needs to respond to ground balls, pop flies, outfield relays, bunts, and baserunners. He also needs to back up the second baseman on throws from the catcher and when the second baseman is fielding, and understand the game to make decisions. This player needs to be one of the strongest players in catching and throwing. The shortstop position is one of the most demanding positions in baseball.

Third baseman: Most right-handed hitters hit in this direction, and a hard batted ball reaches the third baseman quicker than any other position. This player needs to be able to respond quickly, blocking hard hit ground balls, and recover quickly to complete the throw to any base. He needs a strong throwing arm.

Catcher: The catcher is the cornerstone of team defense. This player needs to be adept at blocking balls in the dirt, responding to pop-ups and bunts, and making tag plays at home plate. Size is not as critical as lack of fear in going after the ball in the strike zone or in the dirt when the batter is swinging. This player needs good basic skills and an ability to hustle. Leadership qualities are a plus.

Pitcher: In addition to his responsibilities pitching the ball, the pitcher is an important fielder. The pitcher needs to be aggressive in making as many plays as he can on bunts, weak pop-ups, and balls hit back to him. He backs up third and home with men on base. He also covers first when the first baseman is fielding away from the base.

Rightfielder: The rightfielder needs to track down hit balls and make quick and accurate throws to infielders. He needs to be quick, alert, and have a strong arm in order to stop runners at third base. He also backs up first base.

Centerfielder: The centerfielder is the "captain" of the outfielders. He needs to be able to track down hit balls and make quick and accurate throws to an infielder waiting for the relay throw. He has the most territory to cover and needs to have a strong arm. He backs up second base.

Leftfielder: The leftfielder needs to be able to track down hit balls and make quick accurate throws to the infielders. He receives the most balls and needs to be alert and mentally prepared to make a quick decision about what to do with the ball once he catches it.

Preparing for the Pitch

Getting ready for every pitch, both physically and mentally, is a skill your players need to learn. Take time as often as you need to review ready form with your players. Infielders are closest to the action and need to respond quickly. They want their feet spread slightly wider than their shoulders, knees bent, rear ends down (like they're about to take a seat), hands out in front of the body, and gloves open wide to give the ball the biggest target possible.

Outfielders take a similar position without putting their gloves as close to the ground. An outfielder wants his glove just in front of his knees; a high percentage of all balls fielded by an outfielder will be on the ground.

As players advance in their fielding ability, their anticipation skills will improve. They need to be able to move their feet to position themselves for the incoming ball and to make plays that require lateral or forward/backward movements. A tennis player about to receive a serve is crouched with his feet moving; you want your players using this same technique. Most outstanding catches are the result of the outfielder getting a great first step and read on the direction of the ball.

Upbeat baseball banter is a huge part of the game and keeps fielders alert. Talk and encourage your players—and have them encourage each other. Remind your players how many outs there are, and position them based on the hitter. This keeps them in the game. Teach your players to relax between pitches so that their bodies stay loose. Impress upon them that baseball is a mental sport as well as a physical one.

Communication on Defense

Balls hit in the air that draw two or more defensive players to the catch can present a challenge on every level of baseball. With all eyes focused on the flight of the ball, the potential for a misplay or a collision is a definite possibility. To minimize this problem, you want to have a team approach to handling fly balls. Communication between players will eliminate most problems regarding which player will make the catch. For any ball hit in the air, the player making the catch calls, "Ball, ball, ball!" This tells nearby teammates to allow that player to have right-of-way to the ball.

Team Defensive Rules

- For all balls hit in the air to the outfield, the centerfielder has the right-of-way over the leftfielder and the rightfielder. This means the centerfielder may call for any catch that he has a reasonable chance of making, and the leftfielder and rightfielder give way to his call, "Ball, ball, ball."

- For pop flies in between the outfielders and the infielders, outfielders have the right-of-way over the infielders. Although infielders can make catches moving out toward the outfield, it is easier for outfielders to make catches moving in toward the infield. Again, the outfield would call "ball, ball, ball" to inform his teammates.

- For all balls hit in the air in the infield area, including foul territory, the shortstop and the second baseman, or middle infielders, have the right-of-way over the first and third baseman or corner infielders.

- For all balls hit in the air between first and home or third and home, the corner infielders have the right-of-way over the catcher, including balls in foul territory.

⚾ For balls hit in the air around the pitching mound, the pitcher may make catches on balls that are not hit very high. Otherwise, he helps direct the play by calling the name of the player who is in the best position to make the catch.

Backing Up

A baseball team is just that: a team. One of the best ways a player can help his team is to back up plays. This is a selfless act. Basically, the player backing up acts as insurance in case a ball is misplayed or overthrown, which is quite common in youth baseball. The backup player can prevent extra bases from being taken and prevent runs from being scored. He gives himself as much room as possible to react to the ball, and to make sure the ball cannot get past him. He is the last line of defense! Especially with men on base, all nine players on the field may be moving to make the play on the hit or begin to back up. Backing up comes down to everyone hustling and anticipating what could occur, and putting themselves in position in case it does.

You can walk through some simple backup rotations starting with the most basic ones and adding more as the team gets more experienced.

Teaching Relays

The relay is one of the most exciting team concepts in baseball. In youth baseball, a successful throw from one player to another can be reason for celebration. Adding a second or third in sequence can seem incomprehensible. But if you teach technique, practice composure, and drill execution, your team can conquer this challenge. Building effective relay play is richly rewarding.

Communication is key. The player receiving the ball should raise both hands above his head, start bouncing up and down, and give a verbal cue such as, "Hit me, hit me" in a loud voice. This gives the player throwing the ball a target to hear and see. The throw is not a bullet that is hard to control but an accurate direct throw to the glove side so the player receiving the ball can catch it and already be in throwing position. This will quicken the relay.

The player receiving the throw is aligned in a straight line to the base he anticipates the throw is continuing to. The player covering the base verbally coaches the player catching with consistent directives. Teach commands that are simple and clear. "Cut, second" could mean that the player receiving the throw should catch it and throw to second as the runner is advancing.

In coaching youth baseball, focus on a few common relays and get them down well. You can add to these as the season goes along, but keep in mind, you will gain little from reviewing scenarios that seldom happen.

The size of the Little League fields calls for adjustments to the relay systems used on full-sized fields. The closeness of the outfield fences, the proximity of the outfielders to the infield, and the shorter base paths all impact your younger team's relay system.

Basic Youth Relays

With no one on base, on balls safely hit to the outfield the hitter will aggressively turn toward second base, ready to challenge throws to the infield. Outfield throws to a relay player and then to the base will generally take too much time to prevent the advancement of that runner to second base. Therefore, in this situation, outfielders generally throw directly to second base. On balls hit to left field and centerfield, the second baseman will receive the throw at second. The first baseman and the right fielder will move toward second base to back up the play and hold the hitter to a single. The shortstop moves in the direction of the hit, ready to respond to any ball that gets past the outfielder. The pitcher backs up the play at second base.

On balls hit to centerfield, the same procedure follows with the throw made directly to second base. The pitcher is the primary backup while the first baseman remains at first base and behind the hitter as he makes his turn to advance.

On balls hit to right field, the shortstop covers second base to receive the direct throw while the second baseman moves toward the rightfielder to respond to any balls that get past the rightfielder. The leftfielder backs up the throw to second, as does the pitcher. The first baseman covers first base.

With a runner at second and a base hit to left field, centerfield, or right field, the pitcher will become the cutoff man for all throws to home plate. The *cutoff* is the player who stops the motion of the thrown ball toward home plate. Because the pitcher is one of the best athletes on the field, you want him handling all throws when possible. If the cutoff throw by the pitcher to home plate gets past the catcher, the pitcher moves to cover home plate.

In the case of a ball hit deeply to the outfield that is a definite double or possible triple, the shortstop aligns himself with the direct throw to third base. His distance from the outfield throw is based on the depth of the outfielder making the throw and the strength of the outfielder's arm. The first baseman moves to set up as a possible cutoff person in front of the pitching mound. The pitcher backs up third base. With a runner at first base, the shortstop serves as the cutoff for all throws to third base. Considering that he is probably the best player on the field, you want the shortstop to handle as many plays as possible. His alignment for all throws to third is based on the depth of the throw and the outfielder's arm strength. His decision making on allowing the throw to go to third is based on the runner's position as the play develops. If there is no play at third or if the throw is well off-line, he will cut off the throw and respond to the runner rounding first base.

Most of this makes common sense. Diagram it on paper and you can see the flow. Diagramming it for your players can be valuable as well. They will enjoy the "chalk talk" and it will give them further clarity. The players can take their positions in a smaller area closer together and you can review relays and backups. This allows multiple repetitions in a very short time.

Good teams do not want to beat themselves at any level. Teaching the ability to stay composed, find the cutoff, and execute a good throw will make your team outstanding.

EXPERIENCE TALKS For relays, the distance between the player fielding the ball and person taking the throw varies depending on arm strength. Yankee outfielder Johnny Damon is a great player; his biggest weakness is his arm. When his teammates are receiving a relay throw from him, they go to a position where Damon can reach them.

Drills

1. BARE HAND TOSS

This drill helps players overcome any fear of catching the ball. Players pair up as partners, 6 to 8 feet apart and without gloves, to toss the baseball underhand at varying heights to each other. Align all partners in the same direction to avoid accidents. Encourage catching with relaxed fingers and teach your players

to soften the impact of the ball as it is being caught by drawing the hand back toward the body. This is called *funneling*. Emphasize seeing the ball enter the hand.

DURATION: 2–3 minutes

2. GLOVE TOSS

Set up as in the bare hand toss drill, only now add baseball gloves. Once the ball is caught, players transition to proper throwing position. Emphasize funneling the ball into the midpoint of the body, then moving correctly and not rushing into proper throwing position.

STEP IT UP: Extend the distance to 10 to 15 feet and use an overhand toss.

DURATION: 2–3 minutes

3. ONE HAND GROUNDERS

This drill practices being in the ready position with the glove hand. Set up with gloves on, partners 10 to 15 feet apart. The throwing arm is tucked behind the player's back. The glove hand is in a forward position close to the ground where the player can see the glove and the ball. He moves

his feet slightly to get into position to field the bottom of the ball. Partners toss grounders to each other underhand. Have your players concentrate on watching the ball into their glove, but also seeing their glove with their peripheral vision.

DURATION: 2–3 minutes

4. GROUND BALLS

Set up with gloves on, partners 10 to 15 feet apart. This drill is similar to drill 3, but now both the glove hand and throwing hand are open and in front of the body, with players' feet moving slightly to position to receive the ball. Partners toss grounders to each other underhand, watching the ball into their gloves but also seeing their gloves with their peripheral vision. Players use two hands for the catch and practice getting used to the rhythm of bounced balls, fielding the bottom of the ball, funneling it into the body, then moving to throwing position.

STEP IT UP: When your players are ready, expand this drill by having partners throw 3 to 4 feet to the left and right of each other's starting position and practice squaring the body to keep the ball in front of the fielder.

DURATION: 2–3 minutes

5. FLY BALLS

For this drill, partners are 20 to 25 feet apart, exchanging overhand fly balls. Players are moving their feet to adjust to the ball's location and catching it in front of their body with both hands. On the throw back to his partner, the player is moving his feet and body to keep the arc of the toss in front of him. Start to emphasize quickness in catching and returning the ball, without letting the mechanics break down.

DURATION: 2–3 minutes

6. TEAM LINE DRILL

This drill practices relays, demanding that players use all the fundamentals of throwing, catching, and working together as a team while stressing making plays under pressure. Arrange the team in lines of four or five players stretching from the home plate area to centerfield. Each player is within throwing distance for their ability level from the next one in line. Each team starts with a ball at home plate and throws to the next player in line, until the ball gets to the last player. That player then returns the ball back down the line until the ball goes back to home plate. Repeat the drill, teaching the fundamentals of relay executions. For example, the player receiving the ball has his hands extended in the air and is yelling, "Hit me, hit me" to signal that the player is ready to receive the ball in his glove. Encourage receivers to move their feet to get to the ball, whether that means shuffling, stepping, or running so that if he gets a bad throw, he'll have an easier time reacting to it. Players receiving the ball should catch it on their glove side. This will allow for a fluid transition into throwing position. Throwers should be reminded to focus on accuracy, as errant throws distort the drill and will correlate to errors in games.

STEP IT UP: Once your team gets more proficient, this can be done in a competition as described in the game section at the end of this chapter; competing puts game-intensity pressure on the players to throw and catch well.

DURATION: 6–10 minutes

EXPERIENCE TALKS

While a player who throws with a rocket arm is great and mesmerizes the fans, players with average and even below-average arms can be successful on any level. David Eckstein of the St. Louis Cardinals has a throwing arm well below average, but he has a quick release and his accuracy is superb.

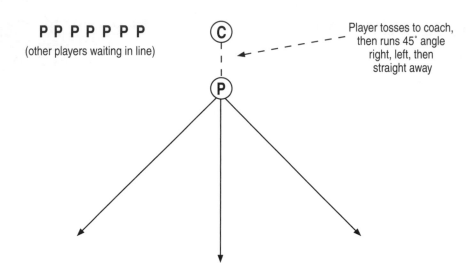

P P P P P P
(other players waiting in line)

Ⓒ

Ⓟ

Player tosses to coach, then runs 45° angle right, left, then straight away

7. FLY BALL ANGLES

This drill is helpful to both infielders and outfielders and is designed to show them how to move away from home plate to receive a pop fly or fly ball. You can set it up in any open area in the outfield. The players form a single line to the right of the coach. The first player, ball in hand, faces the coach at a distance of 10 to 12 feet. To start the drill, he tosses the ball underhand to the coach. Then, beginning with a diagonal step backward, followed by a turn, the player sprints at a 45-degree angle to his right, away from the coach, without looking at the coach. The coach then throws overhand a high fly ball beyond the reach of the fielder. The fielder looks up for the position of the ball while it is in flight. Right-handed players will need to use a backhand position for the catch. Upon catching the ball, the player immediately goes into a strong balanced throwing position and returns the ball accurately in a direct line to the next player at the front of the line. Play continues until every player has had a chance to run that angle.

Next, the line starts again and each player runs the angle to his left, with left-handed players needing to use the backhand position this time.

For the final part of the sequence, the first player in line underhand tosses to the coach, then runs a direct route straight away from the coach. The coach throws the ball beyond the reach of the fielder, who has to adjust to the flight of the ball by looking over his left or right shoulder.

DURATION: 10–12 minutes

8. DIVE

Two cones are placed approximately 6 to 8 feet apart. Players form a single line with the first player in direct line with the two cones. The next player in line will be 2 yards behind his teammate. The purpose of the drill is to improve hand-eye coordination and general reaction to a batted or thrown ball. The first player is in ready position, glove on, both hands open, legs and feet moving as if he's doing a quick, low jog in place. He faces the coach who is

10 feet in front of the cones. To start the drill, the coach throws the ball underhand slightly above the ground just beyond the right cone. With his arm and hand fully extended, the player watches the ball into his glove as he horizontally dives for the catch. Next, go through the line tossing beyond the left cone. If the player misses the catch, he returns to his starting point and tries again. This drill is a good team spirit builder as each player moves into the competitive spotlight.

STEP IT UP: Do the drill with random tosses to the left or right; the player will not know beforehand where the ball is going.

DURATION: 10–12 minutes

WATCH FOR . . . a player not completing a full extension with his arm and hand before diving for a ball. If a player's arm or wrist is bent, this can result in injury. Or if a player doesn't watch the ball into his glove and safeguard it, he may drop the ball upon impact.

9. SQUARE

Line the team up and have players count out one through four. Assign the number ones to go to home plate, the twos to first, the threes to second, and the fours to third. You will need a minimum of eight players to do this drill. One player from each base steps up, with the other players at that base in line behind him. The ball starts at home base and goes counterclockwise so the player at home throws to the player at third. Then that player at home sprints to the end of the line at third. The next player at home steps up to take his place. The player at third catches the ball and throws it to the player covering second. He follows his throw and sprints to the end of the line at second. The drill continues around the bases until everyone has had at least one turn.

This drill demands accuracy of throwing and good receiving skills such as catching with two hands, finding the seams, and proper footwork. Do this drill on a regular basis and your team will improve quickly and confidence will soar. If need be, for very young players, you can position them a few steps in from the bases so the throw is not as far.

STEP IT UP: When you are confident that this drill is being properly executed, you can add a second ball to start at second base. Do the same drill, except twice as fast. This puts pressure on the players to concentrate and to execute. Poor throwing or catching will disrupt the drill.

DURATION: 5–7 minutes

WATCH FOR . . . kids feeling pressure, especially your less talented kids. Make sure the other kids are encouraging! Throwing the ball around the infield is an art form for any team and takes practice, time, and patience to master.

10. POP FLIES AND FLY BALLS

Outfielders and infielders are in normal defensive position. The coach is between the pitching mound and second base. To start the drill, the coach throws balls to various areas in the outfield to simulate game situations. Players respond to the throws according to the rules of defense, communicating to their teammates as they go for the ball.

The coach then moves to home plate to throw pop flies in the infield area, making a point to direct balls in the corner infielders' area and the middle infielders' area.

DURATION: 10–12 minutes

11. DUMMY TEAM DEFENSE

Walkthroughs are invaluable teaching opportunities. This exercise is done by every professional, college, and high school team prior to a game. It can help your players understand where to throw the ball, the importance of backing up their teammates, and just give them a better understanding of how to play the game. Demonstrating to the players where they should go will make your team that much more effective and productive.

All you need is a limited space; no balls are needed as everything is done dry. This can be done while you are waiting for the field prior to practice or incorporated as part of your practice plan. You can cover many simple scenarios that occur during a game at the level you are coaching. Some common backup situations include:

- outfielders backing up infielders on any ground ball
- outfielders backing up each other on fly balls or line drives
- infielders backing up throws from the outfield
- rightfielder backing up first (such as on bunt plays) whenever possible
- centerfielder backing up second on steal situations
- pitchers backing up third and home on base hits to the outfield

There are hundreds of scenarios you can create. What is important is that you prepare your team by selecting some of the most common situations that will occur at your level of play. With repetition, eventually you will see your players react in this drill and begin to transfer their knowledge over to games. You may even ask your kids to come fifteen minutes early before games to walk through different base hit scenarios.

DURATION: 6–10 minutes

12. TEAM RELAY

This is an opportunity for your team to actually play through the type of scenarios they dummied in drill 11. The entire team takes their field positions. Alternate fielders can take a turn once the first player in that position has fielded and thrown. The coach specifies a game situation and then fungoes a ball from the pitcher's mound to each outfielder, starting with left field. According to the situation, the fielder needs to make the appropriate play.

Relay Scenarios	Single to left field
No runner on base	Leftfielder throws directly to second base; second baseman covers second; shortstop moves toward leftfielder to assist; centerfielder backs up leftfielder; rightfielder moves to back up second baseman; pitcher and first baseman back up second baseman; third baseman and catcher hold their positions.
Runner at first base	Shortstop lines up relay for throw to third base; pitcher backs up third base; second baseman covers second base; first baseman covers first base; rightfielder backs up second base; third baseman covers third base; centerfielder backs up leftfielder.
Runners at first and second	Pitcher moves to become relay for direct throw to home plate; basemen cover their bases; shortstop moves toward leftfielder to assist; catcher prepares to receive relay throw; rightfielder backs up second base; centerfielder backs up leftfielder.

13. INFIELD DEFENSE

This drill works specifically on coordinating the reactions and communication between the pitcher, catcher, and infielders. To set up, the pitchers are in foul territory halfway between home plate and first base with the other pitchers lined up one behind the other, perpendicular to the baseline.

Part 1 — Ball hit to the right side of the infield, first or second baseman:
To begin the drill, the first pitcher in line goes to the pitching mound. He throws an imaginary ball to the catcher. As the ball is released, the coach, using a fungoe bat, hits a ground ball toward the first baseman. Upon identifying that the first baseman will handle the ground ball, the pitcher runs a direct route toward first base, placing his right foot on first base with his last step. Upon fielding the ball, the first baseman takes a series

Single to centerfield	Single to right field
Centerfielder throws directly to second base; second baseman covers second; shortstop moves toward centerfielder to assist; leftfielder and rightfielder back up centerfielder; pitcher backs up second baseman; first baseman covers first base; third baseman and catcher hold their positions.	Rightfielder throws directly to second baseman; shortstop covers second base; second baseman moves toward rightfielder to assist; centerfielder backs up rightfielder; leftfielder backs up second base; pitcher backs up second base; first baseman covers first; third baseman and catcher hold their positions.
Shortstop lines up relay for throw to third base; pitcher backs up third base; second baseman covers second base; first baseman covers first base; rightfielder backs up second base; third baseman covers third base; leftfielder backs up centerfielder.	Shortstop lines up relay for throw to third base; pitcher backs up third base; second baseman covers second base; first baseman covers first base; centerfielder backs up rightfielder; leftfielder moves to back up third base; third baseman covers third base.
Pitcher moves to become relay for direct throw to home plate; basemen cover their bases; shortstop moves toward centerfielder to assist; catcher prepares to receive relay throw; rightfielder backs up centerfielder; leftfielder backs up third base.	Pitcher moves to become relay for direct throw to home plate; first and third basemen cover their bases; shortstop covers second base; second baseman moves toward rightfielder to assist; catcher prepares to receive relay throw; centerfielder backs up rightfielder; leftfielder backs up third base.

of two or three steps toward the pitcher covering the base and tosses the pitcher the ball at shoulder height or slightly above to help the pitcher make the catch as he moves to a proper position tagging the bag.

Part 2—Ball hit to the pitcher; runner at first base: This scenario coordinates the pitcher and shortstop in a double play situation. The first pitcher remains on the mound and, again, pitches an imaginary ball to the hitter. Upon the release of the pitch, the coach fungoes a ball directly to the pitcher on the mound. The pitcher fields the ball and throws the ball to the shortstop covering second base to retire the baserunner coming from first. The shortstop then throws to first base to get the runner out and complete the double play. Upon completion of this play, the second pitcher takes the mound and the ball is fungoed to the first baseman, as in Part 1. The drill moves forward with the pitchers rotating in and each taking a turn with each part of the drill.

Part 3—Bunt to third base side of the diamond; runner on second: The goal here is to prevent the runner from reaching third, but the important part of this defensive play is to make sure there is an out somewhere. If the fielders cannot defend the runner at second from going to third, they must get an out at first base. The third baseman controls this play. He wants to position himself before the pitch with his body at a 45-degree angle so he can see the runner at second, while at the same time respond to a bunted ball. This positioning also discourages the runner at second from stealing third. Because it is a potential bunting situation, the third baseman is three to four steps in front of third base toward home plate, away from the foul area. He reads the position of the bunt when it rolls down the third baseline and has the right-of-way over the pitcher. If he anticipates there is no play at third, he lets the pitcher know he is going to field the ball by saying, "Mine, mine, mine." While this drill is being completed, pitcher one jogs back to the end of the line. Next, pitcher two moves to the center of the mound where a ball is fungoed to the pitcher to complete the double play with the shortstop and the first baseman. Once this is completed, pitcher number three moves to the mound and a ball is fungoed in the direction of the third baseman to repeat the drill all the way through.

Part 4—Ball hit to mound; bases loaded: For this drill, the pitchers are behind the mound area in a single line toward second base. Pitcher number one delivers an imaginary pitch to the hitter, then the coach fungoes a ball directly back to the pitcher. The pitcher fields the ball and moves his feet to get into proper throwing position to deliver the ball to the catcher at home plate. The catcher then relays the ball to the first baseman to complete the out.

STEP IT UP: Variations on this same drill can include adding the pitcher's reaction and throw to the catcher with a runner at third base who is not forced and must be tagged out, or adding the pitcher's reaction to a bunted ball somewhere in front of home plate that forces him to receive and relay the ball to the catcher for a tag of the baserunner coming from third.

DURATION: 12–15 minutes

14. CUSTOM TEAM DEFENSE DRILL

Preparing a team for every imaginable situation is the mark of a great coach. You, however, are not coaching a professional team and do not have the practice time to cover the range of plays that could occur; you are coaching kids. So after you've introduced various defensive scenarios, pick out five plays common for your playing level and drill them thoroughly. Make sure everyone knows where to go when the ball is hit to a certain place. Make sure the players know how to react in the event of an error or misplay. Your goal is to make sure the ball is thrown to the correct player with accuracy and to get players to think ahead and know what to do if the ball is hit to them.

STEP IT UP: As your team gets proficient at those five plays, add more plays, increasing the complexity as they learn.

DURATION: 12–15 minutes

GAMES

1. RELAY TEAMS

The basic setup is the same as in drill 5, with four to five players per line lined up between home and centerfield. Different variations can make the action competitive.

Variation 1: One line performs the event timed. When the coach blows the whistle, the first line has to run to the positions (home base to a marker in centerfield) and throw the ball up and back without any errors; the timer stops when the ball reaches home plate. If players miss anywhere along the line, they have to get the ball back to home plate and start over. Then the next line is timed, and the third line is timed while the other two lines watch. The lowest time wins.

Variation 2: All lines perform at the same time. The goal is four times up and back, with no errors. If the ball is dropped, that line has to start completely over. The first line to finish wins.

Variation 3: This one is easiest to keep track of if there is a coach or parent to monitor every line. All lines perform at the same time. As the ball goes up and back, each line gets points: every catch is 1 point; every miss is minus 1 point. If the ball goes up and back without any errors, that's an additional bonus point. Play the game for a set number of minutes and see which team comes out with the most points. Not enough coaches to keep your players honest? Do this one line at a time for a shorter duration while others watch.

CHAPTER 8

LEARNING THE BASICS: PITCHER

The best thing about baseball is that you can do something about yesterday tomorrow.

— MANNY TRILLO

You may have heard this saying: The pitcher's mound is the highest place on the diamond because the pitcher is the most important position. According to Coach Fran O'Brien, this is true. "You have to have pitching to be successful. Pitching is also the most demanding position in baseball, with due respect to position players, and swinging the bat."

So much more than throwing a baseball, pitching is an art that demands the young athlete master the mechanics, the mental awareness, and the mental toughness to deliver results, over and over, while being the very center of attention.

At some point, nearly every young player wants to be pitcher. As the coach, you will be aware that certain players on your team have physical attributes more suited to pitching than others. Arm strength, body strength, height, and mental toughness are all qualities a coach looks for in a pitcher. Do not, however, discourage players whose physical attributes do not suggest pitching success. While you may work to develop one to three of the stronger athletes as pitchers, you can teach every player the mechanics. The balance position and flat back position emphasized in pitching can help all your players understand how to throw the ball correctly. And although a starting player in a youth league may be one of the smallest on the team, his body type may change as a teen and he may become one of the strongest players.

Extremes of Success and Failure

When kids are just learning a sport, success and failure can be quite pronounced. As a coach, one of your responsibilities is to make sure a game does not destroy an athlete. Your encouragement will be one of the main supports allowing these young pitchers to maintain themselves and move forward. You need to prevent a youngster from being humiliated or hurt with what happens in a practice session or game. Control any player's potential humiliation or hurt by addressing the team as a whole and working individually—always encouraging, always continuing to develop the player's skills.

"Our society can put so much emphasis on winning," says Coach Fran O'Brien, "that we can fail to recognize emotional needs. Be sensitive to your pitchers if they're having trouble throwing strikes or giving up hits. Baseball should be a fun game to practice and to play. There may be a losing team according to the score, but *there are no losers in your dugout.*"

Every young athlete, including the pitcher, should feel good about the experience of competing in a baseball game.

WATCH FOR ... all the different ways your young player communicates. Coaching is communication, and perhaps nowhere is this more critical than with your pitcher. Be aware of body language. When the head goes down, the shoulders slump, and the overall body language becomes negative, it's time to go to the mound for a talk. As soon as you get to the mound, make direct eye contact with the athlete and make the first words out of your mouth words of encouragement: "You can; you will; let's get it done." Then you can address one thing that will help the pitcher get past the challenges he's facing. "Whether you're coaching in a youth league, college, or at Fenway Park," says Coach Fran O'Brien, "unless you develop those lines of communication, you're going to get negative results."

Pitching Limits

If pitchers have not mastered the correct mechanics, they are opening themselves up to potential arm and shoulder injury. Even when pitchers are throwing correctly, monitoring the total numbers of innings pitched and the number of pitches thrown is critical to their health and well-being. There is no blanket policy that will cover all pitchers. Age, physical development, and arm strength all factor into the amount of throwing per week any young pitcher can handle. Common sense—and not the next opponent—should dictate the use, and overuse, of each pitcher's arm. This is particularly vital when the pitcher is also a position player. Although winning games is a goal, you certainly don't want to accomplish it at the expense of a young developing athlete.

Little League rules limit the number of innings a pitcher may throw in a six-day period to six. If a pitcher throws more than one inning, he must take three days off from game competition. Many teams stop a pitcher after three innings and bring him back to pitch on three days' rest to pitch three more innings. This will probably result in 60 to 70 game pitches, which is acceptable for the week. The goal is to limit the total number of pitches, including bullpens, to no more than 150 pitches per week. The breakdown of any pitcher's mechanics, like elbow dropping, are indications of arm fatigue.

Bullpen sessions should be monitored as well, once the short-up workout is completed, with no more than 25 to 30 pitches maximum per session.

EXPERIENCE TALKS

With higher-level players, you also need to pay attention to the pitcher's practice rotation. If a pitcher threw last night in a very competitive game, you would not bring him back to practice the next day. He has a day of rest, he does a lot of stretching, and any throwing would only be light toss.

Pitching Mechanics

Starting Position

With both feet in the pitching area (mound), for a right-handed pitcher, the right foot is slightly ahead of the left foot. For a left-handed pitcher, the left foot would be slightly in front. The pitcher is relaxed, confident, and focused. The glove is about chest high with

the back of the glove facing the catcher. The throwing hand with the ball rests comfortably over the pocket of the glove.

Drop-Step and Pivot

The back foot action is simply a small up-and-down lift with the foot coming slightly off the ground. The front foot pivots off the heel: heel turning in, toes out.

High Balance Position

To move into the high balance position, as a right-handed pitcher, the left knee is elevated slightly above the hip area. For the left-handed pitcher, the right knee would be elevated. The front side—head, chin, front shoulder, and hip—are closed in a direct line to the catcher, establishing the *power line*. The lift leg and foot are in a relaxed position. The pitcher does not let his body drift forward prior to the hands separating; this results in the throwing hand being too far behind the body as the stride foot lands and will compromise the release of the pitch.

Low Balance Position

Moving from the high balance position, the lifted leg returns as it comes up (no step forward) to balance just above the ground, maintaining the power line.

Making the Loops

As the hands break in the high balance position, the throwing hand moves down and back with the hand on top of the ball, then up with the elbow above the shoulder to form the correct arm action. This is the first loop. Continuing into the second loop, the throwing hand comes by the head (the elbow is still higher than the shoulder) as the pitcher strides into his finish position. When *the nose is in front of the front toes*, the ball is released in front of the body on a downward plane

with a snap of the wrist. The arm finishes the second loop by coming down and across, below the opposite knee. The first loop is down and up; the second loop is up and down.

Glide to Stride

From the low balance position, slightly above the ground, the leg glides forward across the top of the ground to land on the ball of the foot. This lead foot is in a direct line to the catcher, pointing slightly toward the center of the body in stride landing position. The glove hand is drawn back into the chest area toward the nonpitching arm in a *glove tuck*.

EXPERIENCE TALKS

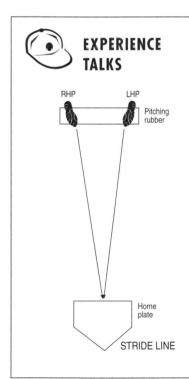

A helpful coaching tool is the *stride line*. This is the line that goes from the toes of the back foot as it rests on the rubber straight to the middle of home plate. The line you actually draw only needs to go just beyond the length of the stride landing position. This line in the dirt gives a guideline for where the pitcher's stride foot should land when he releases the ball. Ideally, the pitcher should land on or near the line. If a right-handed pitcher's stride landing is distinctly right of the line, this blocks the natural throwing motion, compromising the control of the pitch and increasing the possibility of injury. If a right-handed pitcher lands distinctly left of the line, this causes the front side to open too quickly, forcing the throwing elbow below the height of the shoulder, which causes undue stress and prevents the ball from going in a downward plane as it enters the strike zone.

Flat Back Finish

As the front leg lands, the upper torso is directly over the front or stride leg and the hip and backside are released forward, encouraging power generation from the big muscles. In the *finish position*, the back leg and hip are finishing high off the ground; the nose is in front of the toes.

WATCH FOR . . .

Rushing: failure to recognize the balance position and drifting too far forward into a poor release point.

Over-striding: when the pitcher lands his stride on his heel instead of the ball of his foot.

 EXPERIENCE TALKS

"While in junior high school, I developed a better than average curveball," says Coach Fran O'Brien. "It became a very effective pitch. I didn't have a fastball, so I tended to overuse the curveball. As I moved through my high school years, I developed bone chips in my right elbow. The bone chips would lock into the joint of my arm and cause severe pain. By my final year in high school, I was forced to have potentially career-ending surgery on my elbow. Fortunately, I was able to come back, not as a pitcher, but as a position player. Consequently, I never even consider teaching kids younger than high-school age how to throw a curveball. Although it's cool, and sometimes effective, to be able to throw a curveball at a younger age, this can very possibly lead to a long-term injury and impair the child's future as a pitcher."

The Pitches

The two fastballs and the change up (outlined below) can be taught to younger players. When kids are still growing, any arm action that works against the normal or natural function of the joints—particularly the elbow and shoulder area, in the case of pitching—can lead to lasting injuries. After proper physical development (usually high school) with correct instruction, pitchers can learn to throw a curveball correctly, but even then, the curveball should not be overused. With this in mind, specific curveball drills are not included in this teaching series, although any of the throwing drills can be modified to practice this pitch.

Fastball

This is the basic pitch. There are two types of fastballs.

Four-seam fastball: A four-seam fastball is when the player's two fingers are across the baseball where the seams are wide and the thumb is underneath the ball. This produces a reverse rotation on the ball. When the pitcher gets some velocity on the ball, this grip causes the ball to rise over home plate.

Two-seam fastball: A two-seam fastball is when the two fingers are touching the seams where they almost meet and the thumb is underneath the ball. This fastball *runs*, which means as it comes over the strike zone, it moves down.

Change Up

This is when the ball is tucked back into the palm of the hand so the fingertips rise above the contact position on the ball. This creates friction on the ball so when the ball is released with the full arm motion, the ball slows down. The change gives the appearance of a fastball, while actually releasing a pitch that is slower than the hitter is expecting. The pitcher

is literally throwing the hitter off balance. The pitching motion for the change up is exactly the same as the pitching motion for the fast ball.

There are various grips for the change up pitches. The *circle change* is one of the more popular change ups. This grip has the ball tucked in the hand and controlled by the last three fingers, with the thumb and forefinger forming a circle on the side of the ball.

Curveball

The grip for the curveball contacts the seams on the top and bottom of the ball, and can vary. But the pitcher must pull down on the seams while releasing the ball to generate what is called 12-to-6 rotation: the ball is being released at 12 o'clock and ending up at 6 o'clock. To do this pitch, the pitcher begins as if pitching a fastball. As his throwing hand passes the side of his head, the pitcher, reaching up and out, rotates his wrist so the back of his hand turns toward the catcher's mask. Then, with a pulling action on the seams toward his opposite thigh, like a karate chop, he releases the ball.

Drills

When your players are learning to pitch, focus on mechanics, not velocity. Continue to emphasize the positive with constructive teaching and encouragement throughout every practice session. Coaching your players to keep their elbow at shoulder height or higher is critical in developing throwing strength and minimizing the potential for injury. Some of these drills are similar to the throwing drills. The pitching series can also be used to improve your entire team's throwing ability. Include in your practice the drills most suited to your needs.

EXPERIENCE TALKS You don't want to overwhelm your young pitcher, or yourself, by over-coaching: analyzing every play to the smallest detail and figuring out the appropriate follow-up pitch. Here are a few basics to help you coach:

- The four-seam fastball is the easiest for a young pitcher to control—and the pitch he can most rely on for success. In the beginning, don't focus too much on the specific location of the pitch; focus on throwing for strikes.

- The two-seam fastball will have more movement than the four-seam. As a result, it is more difficult to control in the strike zone. Proper repetition and practice can make this pitch more consistent.

- The change up is referred to as a *touch pitch;* getting the proper feel of the grip and the correct release point is more challenging. This pitch is the most difficult of the three, but in the end, it can become the most effective pitch at any level.

For the first six drills, often called *short-up drills,* players are paired up—35 feet apart for beginners, 45 feet apart for more advanced players. Pitching pairs are about 10 feet from other pairs, aligned so that all pitchers are throwing in the same direction. This makes coaching easier and promotes safety. The purpose of the pitching drills is to promote *consistent* mechanics through *constant* repetition. Properly warmed up and stretched, each player delivers three to five consecutive pitches to his partner, who acts as catcher throughout the drills; then they reverse and the partner throws three to five pitches back. Repeat this sequence three to four times for each drill.

1. ONE KNEE

This drill promotes proper arm action for release of the ball; the emphasis is on fluid arm movement. Right-handed players kneel on their right knee with their left knee up; left-handed players reverse this position. Start with the ball clasped in the throwing hand inside the glove—referred to as *ball and glove together.* The front shoulder (left shoulder for a right-hander; right-shoulder for a left-hander) and glove should be pointed toward the target. As the hands separate, the ball is lightly dragged across the top of the grass. The ball hand then swings up to bring the elbow to shoulder height prior to release. The front side remains closed to discourage the elbow from dropping below shoulder height. Upon release of the ball, the upper body moves to a flat back finish.

DURATION: 4–5 minutes

2. SPREAD

This drill practices creating the power line to the flat back finish; the emphasis is on upper body rotation with glove tuck. Partners face each other with feet spread slightly wider than shoulder width and a strong flex in the knee and ankle area. The player rotates his upper body so that the front shoulder and hip are aligned to the target, uses the glove tuck to maintain the power line, and finishes with a flat back.

DURATION: 3–5 minutes

3. HAND BREAK

This drill focuses on understanding the arm action as the ball hand separates, or breaks, from the glove; the emphasis is on making the correct loop as the ball hand moves down and up. The feet are set up as they would be on the pitching mound, ready to pitch. For right-handed players, the right foot would be on the mound parallel to the front edge of home plate, with the left foot also parallel, spread slightly wider than shoulder width. Reverse this for left-handed players. The player's weight is slightly shifted to the back foot. While watching his hands separate, the player completes two consecutive loops to the throwing position. For this drill, he looks back at his hand while making the first two loops; stress that watching the arm is for learning only! On the third loop, now using muscle memory, the pitcher repeats the motion, face forward with eyes on the target, and releases the pitch.

DURATION: 3–4 minutes

4. STRIDE

This drill is for identifying the release point at the completion of the pitching motion; the emphasis is on allowing the hips and back legs to move forward as the player moves to the flat back finish. Start the drill in the stride landing position with most of the weight on the back foot so the player is anchored, his energy stabilized in the hips and back leg in order to generate power into the pitch. Both feet are in the parallel-to-home-plate position, feet slightly spread, ball and glove together. As the hands break and the throwing motion begins, the back hip and leg should be allowed to move forward to generate momentum into a flat back finish. The pitcher does not release the ball until he's into his second loop and his nose is in front of his front foot. Call out comments to your players throughout the drill to clarify the movement; older players can call out to their partners, reminding each other of the focus of the drill.

DURATION: 3–4 minutes

5. HIGH/LOW BALANCE

The first part of this drill is for your players to understand the balance position in pitching and to keep their upper bodies from drifting forward prior to their hands separating. The player starts in the pivot position Having already rotated the lead foot to the front of the rubber, he moves his front or lead knee up to the high balance position. As the hands separate, the front foot moves straight down into the low balance position then glides to the correct landing position, and the pitch is released. The action of this drill is the slow motion used to identify this high balance position and to understand the front leg movement from the high balance to the low balance position, where the foot balances just above the ground in the same place it left.

For the second part of the drill, have the player move into the high balance position, then into low balance position. He repeats this movement two consecutive times without breaking his hands before releasing the pitch. On the third move, the pitcher completes the throw by gliding to home plate slightly above the height of the mound. Include a strong flat back finish.

DURATION: 6–8 minutes

6. GLIDE TO STRIDE

This drill practices engaging the hips and legs in the pitch; the emphasis is on creating power to generate hand speed and arm action. The player starts in the pivot position with the front leg in the low balance position. Front foot toes can lightly contact the ground to help maintain balance. The player glides his front foot slightly above the ground parallel to home plate as his hands separate; his hips and back leg move forward as the pitch is released. He finishes with hips and back leg high, in the flat back finish position. You want the pitcher to glide to the correct landing position without pushing off the back leg. The finished position is a squared-up position where, after release of the ball, the pitcher is directly facing the hitter with feet spread, ready to react to the batted ball.

DURATION: 3–5 minutes

WATCH FOR . . . pushing off that back leg. Everyone talks about the legs with pitching because of the need to use the large muscles in the legs to generate power. However, one of the miscues you hear on neighborhood fields is coaches encouraging players to *push off the rubber*. This is one of the most detrimental coaching tips a coach can give a young player learning to pitch. If a player pushes off with his back foot, he will find it almost impossible to get into the low balance position. Consequently, he will over-stride, landing on his heel in an incorrect position to release the ball.

7. LONG TOSS

This drill develops arm strength; the emphasis is on using the pitching motion to generate hand speed and arm action while throwing the ball from a distance.

 EXPERIENCE TALKS Long toss is not done enough with young pitchers, and can also be quite helpful for position players. Position players could do this drill on a regular basis; pitchers would not do this drill more than two times a week, and, if they pitched one day, they would not long toss the next.

Partners face each other, 10 to 15 feet apart for elementary school players, up to 70 feet apart for advanced pitchers. Pitchers want to create momentum toward their partner. To do this, as each player receives the ball from his partner, he takes a series of small steps in the direction of the target, then releases the ball with proper pitching form. Players want to maintain proper pitching mechanics, throwing on as flat an arc as possible. Players start at a comfortable distance apart, and can then extend the distance up to 120 feet.

DURATION: 10–12 minutes (occasional practices; not daily)

Pitcher's Workout Rotation

For Group II level players getting ready to take on pitching responsibilities, use the short-up drills, the long toss, the shuttle run, and stretching on a regular basis with exercise number one for bullpen series days.

For Group III level players, making this five-day rotation standard practice for all your pitchers can greatly help them improve and develop. Keep in mind that this series is for a designated pitcher. If your pitcher also hits and plays—say, first base—you would back off the training schedule accordingly to ensure the player does not overuse his arm.

DAY 1—SHORT UP

After stretching and warm-up with the team, two pitchers partner up and do the short-up drills. Evaluate your players' needs and have them do all the drills, or just emphasize certain drills. As much as possible, these drills should be supervised. Then have your pitchers long toss. Next is the shuttle run (described below), which is designed to improve overall body conditioning and build leg strength. Conclude the physical workout for the day with side-by-sides (outlined below). Finish the physical workout with stretching.

Shuttle run: Set up an area where three separate distances can be marked from a starting point with cones. For Group II ages, the first distance is 5 yards away, the second distance is 10 yards away, the third distance is 15 yards away; for Group III ages, the first distances is 10 yards away, the second distance is 20 yards away, the third distance is 30 yards away. At your direction, the first player sprints to the first cone and returns to the starting line, then to the second cone and returns, then to the third cone and back—all without stopping. You can vary the intensity and the number of shuttle runs to be completed. A good way to conclude is to have two players running at the same time and competing against one another, with the rest of the team enthusiastically enjoying the competition.

Side-by-sides: Two players work together, one on one knee approximately 5 feet from his partner with two balls available; the other directly facing in a ready position. The first ball is rolled approximately 3 to 4 feet to the left of the ready partner. The ready partner fields the ball with both hands and returns it with an underhand toss. The next ball is rolled 3 to 4 feet to the right of the ready partner and returned with an underhand toss. This is one side-by-side. The drill is ongoing with no stopping in between tosses so the player is moving continually from side to side. When the side-by-side is completed, the players reverse positions and the drill continues.

 EXPERIENCE TALKS Depending on your age group, you can determine how many side-by-sides is a set for your group. For Group II, three sides-by-sides is probably enough for one set. For Group III, five side-by-sides is probably enough for one set.

Stretching: Simple stretching exercises can be done using fenced areas of the field, like the backstop and any sideline fences available. Hold all stretches for 10 seconds. For the first stretch, the player holds onto the fence at about shoulder level—feet together, 2 to 3 feet from the fence—so the player has to lean forward while keeping heels on the ground and stretching the backs of the legs. Next, while still holding onto the fence, move the left foot forward into a bent knee position while keeping the right heel down to stretch the right calf. Reverse legs and stretch the left calf. Continue to hold the fence at shoulder level. Now, the player leans back to stretch shoulders and upper back. Next, relocate the hands on the fence so they are at about waist level. Bend both knees until almost sitting.

Lean back to stretch the lower back area. Next, the player stands so the right hand and arm are extended to the fence with the left shoulder facing away. Gently stretch the right arm: the biceps, triceps, and shoulder. Reverse the position and stretch again. Last, while standing, extend both arms over the head and interlock the fingers in a reverse grip. Extend the arms up and push for the stretch. Stretching before any physical exercise is critical, but stretching afterward is more critical to minimize injury and recovery time. Finally, each pitcher ices his arm and shoulder for a minimum of 15 minutes.

DAY 2—BULLPEN

The bullpen series simulates pitching a game. Use it once a week for any given pitcher; the ideal day is two days before he pitches, giving him one day for his arm to recuperate. The goal is to give pitchers the opportunity to transfer what they've been learning in drills into a game situation. Even at the college level, says Coach Fran O'Brien, every pitch these players use comes out of this bullpen series practice. The total number of pitches thrown in this series depends on the pitcher's physical arm condition on that day and on the number of pitches he needs to get ready to throw in two days. What you are encouraging in the bullpen series is throwing pitches for strikes, using different pitches, and using both sides of the plate. As the pitcher peaks in this series, you should see at least a couple pitches at game speed velocity.

After proper warm-up and stretching, players do the one knee drill and the spread drill for 3 minutes, pitching and catching for an imaginary

EXPERIENCE TALKS

Communication between the pitcher, catcher, and coach is an ongoing process. When you think your players are advanced enough, continue a dialogue between innings so the players can begin learning to make their own game decisions. The foundation for this dialogue is the bullpen drills that are done on a regular basis with coach, catcher, and pitcher. You want consistency in terminology and approach; make sure the same coach works with the pitchers every day.

hitter. Then the pitcher and catcher long toss for 3 to 5 minutes, with the catcher standing in the home plate area while the pitcher moves 10 to 15 feet behind the pitching mound.

Group II—Bullpen Series

1. Using a complete pitching motion, the pitcher throws until achieving five fastballs for strikes.

Group III—Bullpen Series

1. Using a complete pitching motion, the pitcher throws until achieving five fastballs for strikes.

2. To a right-handed hitter, the pitcher throws until achieving two pitches for strikes on the inside (closer to the hitter) and one on the outside (away from hitter).

3. To a left-handed hitter, the pitcher throws to achieve two strikes inside and two strikes outside.

4. The pitcher throws to achieve three change ups for strikes.

5. To a right-handed hitter, the pitcher throws one fastball in, two change ups away.

6. Repeat to a left-handed hitter: one fastball in; two change ups away.

7. Repeat steps 5 and 6 one more time for a right-handed hitter, then a left-handed hitter.

 EXPERIENCE TALKS Mastering the fastball and the change up is not easy. During the bullpen series, you, as coach, want to make evaluations on the strengths of the pitcher and his ability to deliver certain pitches in a game situation. But, particularly at a younger age, because a pitcher has not mastered a change up or a two-seam fastball does not mean he should not work with it. With proper repetition and instruction, the pitcher can bring this into his repertoire. The worst thing you can announce to a young pitcher is that he can't do a particular pitch and shouldn't try.

8. This is a no count, 0–0. Allow the pitcher to pitch against a right-handed hitter first and a left-handed hitter second, with the goal of throwing a strike with the first pitch.

Finish this workout with the stretching sequence and icing the arm and shoulder for 15 minutes.

DAY 3—LIGHT TOSS

The day before a game, your pitcher may want to do some light tossing, or he might not—depending how he's feeling physically.

DAY 4—GAME

After a general warm-up, the pitcher does a 10- to 12-minute pitching warm-up by beginning the bullpen series and continuing through the sequences until he feels ready to walk out on the mound. After the game, the pitcher stretches and ices his arm and shoulder.

DAY 5—LIGHT TOSS

Light tossing on this day can help the pitcher's arm recover. The routine here is the same as day 3, with the addition of stretching exercises and icing the arm and shoulder.

Games

1. TARGET PRACTICE

Pitchers will enjoy a pitching target that hangs on a fence or backstop. Let them have some fun practicing to hit the marks.

DURATION: 10 minutes

CHAPTER 9

LEARNING THE BASICS: CATCHER

A good catcher is the quarterback, the carburetor, the lead dog, the pulse taker, the traffic cop and sometimes a lot of unprintable things, but no team gets very far without one.

— MILLER HUGGINS

There is no more important defensive position on a baseball team than that of catcher. The catcher is involved in every pitch that is thrown, responds to every batted ball, and initiates the team defense that prevents baserunners from stealing and scoring.

There is likely more than one player on your team who could be your catcher, and you want to encourage a few team members to practice for this position. Coaches of younger players are looking for a player who is fearless, has a strong body, and possesses strong hand–eye coordination. Because most kids are right-handed hitters, you want your catcher to be right-handed. A left-handed catcher will find right-handed hitters an obstacle as he attempts to throw to second base. A right-handed catcher has the same difficulty with left-handed batters, but this match-up occurs much less often. Coaches of Group III players also want to look for a catcher with leadership potential, good communication skills, and mental toughness.

One of the biggest attributes a young catcher will show is an enthusiasm for catching. You'll know this by the way he moves around the catching area. Catchers who are active around home plate—scrambling after loose balls in the dirt, hustling after pop-ups—set the tone for the whole game. On any level, your catcher needs to understand how he affects the tone of the game.

To start, you want your catcher sprinting from the dugout to home plate. After receiving the pitch, he delivers the ball back to the pitcher quickly; no lobbing. When the catcher is quick with returns, the pitcher and fielders are more likely to stay ready to play their positions.

Equipment Routine

Designate the proper place for the equipment in the dugout and stress to your catchers that misplacing or mistreating the equipment can hold up the whole game; if the next catcher can't find the left shin guard, everybody waits. If the catcher is not hitting, as the second out of the inning is made, he begins the process of putting on his equipment. In the event the catcher is a baserunner or hitter, at two outs, one of the coaches or backup players needs to go to home plate to help the pitcher warm up for the next inning and give the catcher time to put his equipment on. This stand-in catcher, although not attired to catch, needs to wear a catcher's mask.

Catching Mechanics

Receiving Stance

To receive the pitch, the player's feet are spread beyond the width of the shoulders, with weight on the balls of the feet and the left foot slightly in front of the right foot. In a low crouched position, the player leans forward with his buttocks slightly raised. The glove arm is extended forward, with the elbow slightly bent; the glove is up, in a vertical position, with the glove pocket providing a visible target for the pitcher. Before the pitch is thrown, the catcher may move this target by slightly swaying the upper body in or away from the hitter. His throwing hand is on the side of his right thigh to protect it from being hit by foul balls.

Framing the Pitch

The catcher uses this technique to position his glove before receiving a pitch in or close to the strike zone to encourage a favorable call by the umpire.

- For pitches coming in on the inner side of the plate (for a right-handed hitter), the glove hand is rotated from a vertical position slightly to the left.

- For pitches coming in on the outside of the plate, the glove hand is rotated slightly to the right to catch the outside of the ball.

- For pitches thrown to the bottom of the strike zone, the glove hand is rotated strongly to the left, allowing the glove hand to move slightly under the pitch.

The goal is for the catcher's glove hand to move as little as possible upon receiving the ball, to increase the opportunity to get more strikes called by the umpire.

Throwing Position

Catchers need to be able to move quickly out of receiving position into throwing position. This is particularly important with runners on base where stealing and pickoff opportunities are present. To move from receiving to throwing, the catcher quickly shifts his feet and rises to a crouched stance with legs slightly bent. His front shoulder and hip are aligned to the target in a closed power position. His ball and glove are together at shoulder height. For balls thrown to the left side of home plate, the catcher sweeps the ball across his upper body into throwing position. For balls thrown to the

right side of home plate, the catcher rotates the glove to the right for the catch while shifting his feet and legs to the throwing position.

Blocking Technique

Blocking errant pitches that bounce at or around home plate is an important skill. A catcher who is successful at blocking can prevent baserunners from advancing or even scoring a run. As the catcher recognizes the ball

will bounce in the dirt, he thrusts both knees to the ground, shoulder width apart. He brings his glove and throwing hand quickly between the knees, preventing the ball from getting underneath the body, curls his shoulders forward to keep the ball contained in front of him, and tucks his chin to bring his face mask down to the chest area. Make sure your players practice this chin tuck; it protects them from getting hit by a ball in the throat.

As a catcher recognizes the ball will bounce to his left, he quickly moves his left foot to the outside of the bounced ball while moving his right foot into a basic blocking position. His left shoulder rotates inward to keep the ball in front of the body. For a ball bouncing to his right, the position is reversed.

Once the pitch is blocked, the catcher must recover the ball quickly to prevent baserunners from advancing. As the ball is retrieved, the catcher moves his feet and body into throwing position and, unless the play is at home plate, removes his mask and discards it so he can become a fielder on the play.

Catching Pop Flies

Catching pop flies around the home plate area of the infield is about understanding the right-of-way that defensive players have.

- For pop flies falling somewhere between the catcher and the infielders, the first baseman and the third baseman have the right-of-way over the catcher. Because everyone's head is looking up, your players need to communicate, shouting "Ball, ball, ball!" Remind your players often to call out to each other, and you will hopefully reduce collisions and avoid plays where everyone thinks someone else is catching the ball.

- The catcher has the right-of-way on balls moving in angles toward the backstop, bench, or dugout area. Because of the rotation and spin on the pitches, pop flies here will often look like they're going out of play and then spin and rotate back into the play area before landing. To catch a pop fly, the catcher, upon identifying that the ball is up in the air, discards his mask anywhere it will not be an obstacle for

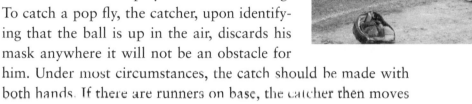

him. Under most circumstances, the catch should be made with both hands. If there are runners on base, the catcher then moves to throwing position.

Giving Signs

Beginning at the Little League level, the catcher takes on the responsibility of signing the pitch. The coach signs to the catcher prior to each pitch, indicating what pitch he wants thrown; the catcher uses signs to relay this information to the pitcher.

The catcher is in a squatting position with legs slightly spread and knees forward when he gives signs. His glove hand and arm are extended just outside the left knee, with his glove vertical to the ground so the opposition doesn't see the signs being relayed to the pitcher. The catcher signs with his right hand, fingers facing down between his thighs and close to the pelvic area—and not below, or the other team can see the sign and

may pick up on which pitch is about to be thrown! Your team will have its own set of signs. Here is a possible sequence:

Coach's Signs

> *Four-seam fastball:* touch your chin
> *Two-seam fastball:* touch your nose
> *Change up:* touch the throat

Catcher's Signs

> *Four-seam fastball:* one finger down
> *Two-seam fastball:* two fingers down
> *Change up:* three fingers down

The position of the ball can also be signed after the sign for the pitch.

Coach's Signs

> *Pitch to inside of plate for right-handed hitter; outside for left-handed:* left hand touches left ear
>
> *Pitch to outside of plate for right-handed hitter; inside for left-handed:* left hand touches right shoulder

Catcher's Signs

Pitch to inside of plate for right-handed hitter; outside for left-handed: thumb down

Pitch to outside of plate for right-handed hitter; inside for left-handed: wiggle little finger

Pickoff Throws

Mishandled pickoffs are one of the most common, and most frustrating, errors you'll see your young players struggle with.

How do you teach a young catcher when to throw for the out and when to hold the ball? A catcher should automatically always be looking for an opportunity to pick a runner off at any base. He should not, however, always be finishing with a throw to an infielder. The concept you want him to understand is how to recognize when he has the advantage and needs to throw; and when he doesn't have the advantage and needs to hold that ball!

He follows through with a pickoff throw only when he sees obvious separation—a space of daylight between the baserunner and the infielders. That's when the infielder has the advantage. When there is no obvious separation, he should not throw to the infielder; when the runner is that close to the base, the runner has

the advantage. If a baserunner is careless about getting back to the base, the catcher needs to be ready to respond with a hard, accurate throw to the base.

Throw to first base: First is the easiest base for your catcher to make a pickoff play with a right-handed hitter because he has open vision to first base.

Throw to second base: Pickoff throws to second base are the hardest; this is the longest throw and demands a strong arm and coordination with middle infielders. Make sure the catcher has a large advantage if he's going to try a pickoff play at second.

Throw to third base: On a pickoff to third base, the third baseman places himself in a visible position inside the diamond, close to third base, so the catcher's throwing angle is not blocked by the baserunner moving back toward third base. If the third baseman is out of position, a throw to him can hit the runner or be misplayed into the left field area. If the third baseman is not visible in this position, the catcher should not throw the ball.

Receive at home plate: To receive throws at home plate for the purpose of tagging the runner out, the catcher places himself in a position slightly in front of home plate with the left foot close to the front edge of the plate. The catcher cannot stand in front of home plate in a direct line with the runner coming from third base unless he has the baseball. If he stands in a direct line without the baseball, this is obstructing, and on contact, the runner is awarded the base.

As the catcher receives the ball, he will slide his left foot and leg to the third-base side of home plate, bringing his glove hand down into a tagging position. This helps block the slide of the runner into home plate, preventing the runner from scoring. Teach your catchers to make this tag with the ball securely in the glove upon impact with the baserunner, so the ball doesn't go flying out of their mitt. Once this play is completed, the catcher immediately moves to a strong throwing position if there are other baserunners to prevent them from taking another base.

 EXPERIENCE TALKS Coach Fran O'Brien had one season where he didn't have either his starting catcher or his reserve catcher able to play for almost two weeks. "Needless to say, this had a very disastrous effect. Catchers really set the tone for the whole team."

Drills

These catching drills require that a coach work with catchers in full equipment. If you do not have anyone assisting you, have your catchers come early or stay later so you can work with them individually. For drill 3, have one of the other catchers play the second baseman; drill 7 includes pitchers.

The length of time allocated for these drills will vary according to the catcher's arm health on a given day. Don't beat your catchers into the ground with drills. Especially with young players, some days you might just do the first two drills; on other days, you might review the first two, and add one more. In practice, and in games, rotate different players into this position. This will help if you have an absence due to injury, illness, or personal emergency that prevents your regular catcher from playing. This is a fun position to teach—and you want it to be a fun position to play.

1. BARE HAND FRAME

This drill practices correct glove hand position when receiving pitches on both sides of the plate. The coach sets up with six to eight balls, 6 to 8 feet away from the catcher. Using his bare hand, the catcher sets up in the receiving position. The coach tosses underhand to the catcher in the strike zone. The tosses are alternated from one side of the plate to the other. The catcher continues to frame the pitch, discarding the ball quickly to his side prior to the next pitch being thrown. Make sure your catcher frames the pitch by catching the outside of the ball and holding the frame for 2 seconds.

DURATION: 6–10 minutes

2. GLOVE FRAME

This drill introduces framing the pitch with the correct glove position. The catcher is in receiving position with the coach 15 to 20 feet from home plate. The coach throws overhand to simulate a pitched ball. The catcher reacts to the pitch by framing balls within the strike zone. The catcher discards received balls prior to the next pitch being thrown. Finish this drill with six consecutive pitches thrown at a rapid pace.

DURATION: 6–10 minutes

WATCH FOR . . . your catcher's receiving arm always being slightly flexed as the pitch enters the glove. This prevents jabbing at the ball.

3. FRAME AND THROW

This drill practices transitioning from the catch and frame position to the throwing position. The catcher starts in the receiving position. The coach, from a distance of 30 to 40 feet, pitches the ball to the catcher. For pitches in the strike zone, the catcher first frames and catches the ball, then quickly shifts to the throwing position. For pitches out of the strike zone, the catcher secures the ball and quickly shifts to the throwing position. Once in the throwing position, the catcher releases the ball to a player at second base.

DURATION: 6–10 minutes

WATCH FOR . . . your catcher rushing the catch, frame, and throw transition. Insist that the catcher get in the correct throwing position before releasing the ball.

4. BLOCKING TECHNIQUE

This drill involves using the correct blocking position for pitches bounced into the strike zone. The catcher is in full equipment in the receiving position. The coach, from a distance of 10 to 15 feet, throws tennis balls to the various blocking positions. Using glove and equipment, the catcher will deflect the balls with the correct blocking technique. Emphasize the foot shifting to block the pitches, and keeping the ball in front of the body.

DURATION: 6–10 minutes

5. BLOCK AND RECOVER

This drill is a progression of drill 4, now using baseballs and encouraging quickness and agility as your catcher recovers the balls.

DURATION: 6–10 minutes

6. BLOCK AND THROW

This drill is the next progression of the action in drills 4 and 5; now the catcher continues and shifts into throwing position. The emphasis now is on the catcher getting into correct throwing position quickly, but still not rushing the throw.

DURATION: 6–10 minutes

7. WILD THROWS

The first priority for the catcher at home base is to prevent the runner at third from scoring. Balls thrown past the catcher are a regular part of the game. This drill helps the catcher practice sliding to the ball to prevent overrunning and mishandling the ball on the ground.

To set up, the pitchers are lined up in front of the mound; the catchers are all in full equipment with the first catcher behind home plate. With the first pitcher and catcher ready, the coach throws a ball in the dirt toward the backstop. As the catcher retrieves the wild throw, the pitcher moves to the front of home plate where he can receive the throw and complete the tag. Once the catcher has the ball under control, he balances on his right knee while elevating his left knee to the throwing position and makes a quick, short throw to the pitcher.

Continue the drill by varying the location of the wild throws to create different angles for the pitcher and catcher pairs to respond to, making sure all the pairs recover balls in different areas.

DURATION: 10–15 minutes

8. THROWING

This sequence reinforces proper throwing skills and develops arm strength. For this drill, two catchers in full equipment are throwing back and forth to each other. Each section is timed for 1 to 3 minutes, depending upon the physical condition of the catchers.

1. Catchers start on their knees facing each other, 25 feet apart for beginners and 30 feet apart for more advanced players. Using the correct throwing motion, they rotate the upper body to create the power line prior to releasing the ball to their partner. Focus on moving the glove hand and ball quickly from the catching position to the throwing position and making sure the elbow is above the shoulder.

2. Catchers face each other at an extended distance, 25 to 65 feet depending upon skill and age level. As the ball is received from the partner, catchers shift to the correct throwing position before releasing the ball with correct form.

3. Catchers set up at a distance that represents a throw made from home to second base. The catcher receives the ball, then sets up in the correct receiving position before throwing the ball, simulating the frame and throw transition at game-level speed.

4. Catchers set up at a distance beyond the normal throw from home to second base. Following the same procedure as in the previous section, the catchers complete this drill with a limited number of extended throws (no more than ten to fifteen) to help develop their arm strength.

DURATION: 6–10 minutes

9. PREGAME DRILL

During batting practice prior to a game, have the catcher in full equipment in the third base area reacting to batted balls from hitters to improve footwork and hand–eye coordination.

DURATION: 5 minutes

Games

1. CHALLENGE

In full equipment, the young catcher challenges his teammates, standing about 10 to 15 feet away, to throw balls at him one at a time. The goal is to see how many consecutive throws he can block or keep in front of himself, in one minute.

DURATION: 1 minute

2. ROCKET

The coach sets up with a bat and ten balls about 45 feet away from the more advanced catcher, who is positioned against a proper screen or fence. The coach hits the balls to the catcher to simulate balls in the dirt. Some of these balls will bounce in front of the catcher; some will be line drives; some will be ground balls. The goal is to see how many consecutive balls a catcher can block at a velocity close to game level. He doesn't need to catch the ball for it to count; he needs to stop it and keep it from going behind him. Give each catcher two attempts at ten balls and see who comes up with the most consecutive blocked balls.

DURATION: 4–6 minutes

CHAPTER 10

LEARNING THE BASICS: BUNTING

It may sound silly, but I don't hear a thing when I'm up at bat. Someone can be standing and hollering right by the dugout, but I don't hear it. I'm concentrating on the pitcher.

—HANK AARON

What is bunting? Bunting is tapping the ball low in the infield as far away from the infielders as possible. When done correctly, the bunt forces the infielders to move out of their best defensive positions to respond to the ball. Bunting is both a skill and an art.

An offensive team decides to bunt to move a runner or runners into scoring position; to break the rhythm of an opposing pitcher that is dominating the game; to take advantage of slower defenders at first or third; or when a weak hitter is up to bat.

Bunting is basically allowing the bat to catch the ball so the ball stays on the ground close to the hitter. This is a skill that can be introduced to Group II level players once or twice a week in practice. With Group III, regular practice will help your players master this skill. Players are not only learning how to do the actual bunt motion; they are also learning how to direct the bunted ball where they want it to go—and to achieve this under game pressure.

Basic Bunting Mechanics

All bunts begin in hitting position. The footwork changes depending upon the bunt, but the hand position remains similar. Basically, to bunt the player is going to slide his hands toward the center of the bat so he can bring the bat out in front to contact the pitch, as described below.

1. The right-handed hitter slides his right hand toward the middle of the bat, around the label, keeping his fingers from wrapping around the bat so they don't contact the pitched ball. The left-handed hitter slides his left hand toward the middle. He also moves his bottom hand up, about 2 to 4 inches away from the knob end of the bat. The tension on the bottom grip is lighter to help deaden the impact of the ball when it hits—and consequently shorten the distance the ball travels.

2. The hitter then brings the bat over the top of the strike zone, extending the bat and his arms toward the pitcher at the top of the strike zone, ready to contact the pitch. He lowers his head and eyes to the top of the strike zone. This puts him in position to look over the top of the bat and follow the path of the ball more clearly. If he stands with head and eyes higher, the hitter is looking down at the ball—which makes getting the ball safely on the ground more difficult.

3. Upon impact of the ball, the bunter gives slightly.

Types of Bunts

Sacrifice Bunt

This is the first type of bunt to teach. The purpose of this bunt is to advance the baserunners to the next base in exchange for the hitter being thrown out. This bunt is directed toward the first or third baseline to draw the baseman away from his base to field the ball, preventing a play being made on the runner. The bunter starts in the batting position, then pivots both feet in the direction of the pitcher as he brings the bat over the strike zone and holds it in front of him. The best area to place the bunted ball in a sacrifice situation is 12 to 15 feet down either baseline. The right-handed player will find it easier to bunt toward first base; the left-handed player will find it easier to bunt toward third. Once the ball is bunted, the hitter becomes a baserunner. His job is an all-out hustle to first that helps create pressure on the throw and catch to first base.

Drag Bunt

The purpose of a drag bunt is to get the hitter to first base. It is also directed toward the first baseline or third baseline. To do the bunt correctly, the player needs to finish the bunt before starting to run to first. As the pitch is delivered, the bunters turn at the last possible moment for an element of surprise. For a right-handed hitter, the bunter makes a short jab step forward with the left foot, followed by pivoting his feet toward the pitcher and moving the bat over the top of the strike zone into proper position. A left-handed hitter reverses this.

Push Bunt

The purpose of the push bunt is to push the ball past the pitcher toward the second baseman, forcing the first baseman to move off the base and cover the play. This bunt is only done by a right-handed hitter, because the momentum of the hitter's feet has him already moving toward first base as he makes contact with the ball. The bat, again, is brought up and over the strike zone and

EXPERIENCE TALKS Ideally, the best place to make contact with the ball is the last few inches at the end of the bat, above the sweet spot. This area deadens the ball and heightens control of the distance the ball will travel. This takes a lot of practice and you shouldn't expect players to master this until high school.

out in front, with the player taking a few short steps in the direction he wants the bunt to go.

Slash Bunt

The slash bunt is more advanced. It is used when the first and third basemen are breaking early to the plate before the pitch to prevent baserunners from advancing. The player purposely puts his bat in a bunt position prior to the release of the pitch. As soon as the pitcher releases the ball, the hitter immediately moves the bat back into hitting position. Then, moving both his hands to grip the bat about 4 to 5 inches higher than normal batting position, he hits the pitched ball with a slashing motion downward, landing the ball on the ground.

Basic Bunting Plays

The object of a squeeze play is to surprise the team on defense as the pitch is being thrown, resulting in a run scoring. A bunter needs enough control to get the ball on the ground but avoid placing the ball near the pitcher, for the pitcher is in the best position to throw to any base for a force out. Make sure the hitter and the baserunner do not give the play away by either the hitter turning too early or the baserunner leaving too early.

Suicide Squeeze

The hitter uses a sacrifice or drag bunt to place the ball in front of home plate to create a difficult play for the pitcher and infielders. It's called a *suicide* because once the play is in motion, there is no turning back: if the play doesn't work, it will result in an out. With a set sign from the coach, the runner at third is moving with the pitch and the hitter is reacting to the ball as it leaves the pitcher's hands. The hitter must attempt to bunt the hit regardless of the location of the pitch.

Safety Squeeze

On a safety squeeze, the player doesn't have to hit if the pitch is out of the strike zone. At a signal from the coach, the runner at third reacts to the bunt play, but unless he has an advantage, he doesn't have to continue to home plate.

Bunting for a Base Hit

Bunting may be used to get a runner on first, especially if the bunter is a fast runner. A right-handed hitter can use a drag or push bunt; a left-handed hitter can sacrifice a bunt down the third baseline. If you're thinking about calling a bunt play for a base hit, look for the first and third basemen to be playing even with the bag, or behind.

Drills

1. BUNTING POSITION

Players are lined up in front of the coach, bat in hand. The coach introduces and demonstrates the correct technique for a sacrifice bunt. The players follow and the coach walks around and adjusts.

STEP IT UP: Individually introduce drag bunting, push bunting, or slash bunting in the same classroom manner.

DURATION: 5 minutes

2. BUNTING PRACTICE

Divide the players into three groups. Group 1 is at home plate with bat and helmet. Players from Groups 2 and 3 are in the infield with their mitts retrieving balls and returning them to the bucket. The coach is about 10 feet in front of the pitching mound with a bucket of balls. Each player takes a turn at the plate to practice bunting, receiving a minimum of three pitches. Depending upon ability level, the coach can choose an underhand or overhand pitch. The groups rotate, each taking a turn at home plate. Correct the mechanics of your players during the drill so they are improving their bunting technique.

STEP IT UP: Expand drill to practice drag bunting, push bunting, and slash bunting.

DURATION: 10–12 minutes

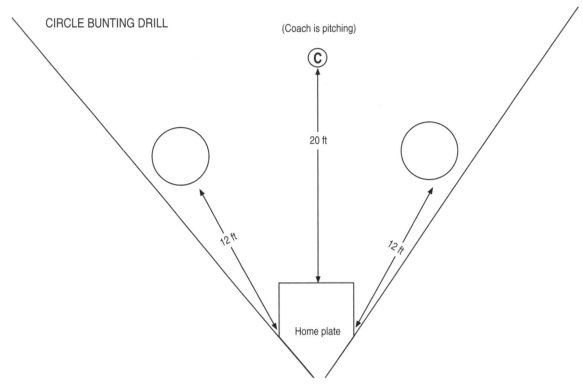

CIRCLE BUNTING DRILL

(Coach is pitching)

C

20 ft

12 ft

12 ft

Home plate

3. CIRCLES

Draw two large circles approximately 3 to 4 feet in diameter: One circle is 12 to 15 feet from home plate toward the third baseline; the other circle is 12 to 15 feet toward the first baseline. Each hitter will be given four pitches to locate the bunted ball in or around the circle. The coach designates where the bunts should go: two toward first base, two toward third base, or alternate. Leave balls that land in the circle in place to instill some competitive spirit in the players to follow.

DURATION: 12–15 minutes

4. SQUEEZE BUNT

This drill not only teaches correct bunting technique, but also introduces the third baserunner to his responsibilities. Divide the team into three groups: one group is at home getting ready to bunt; one group is at third base getting ready to react to the bunt; the third group is in the infield to retrieve the baseballs and bring them back to the mound area. The coach is about 10 feet in front of the pitcher's mound with a bucket of baseballs. The coach pitches overhand, the batter bunts, and the runner leaves third. Once everyone in the first group has bunted, rotate twice so everyone gets a chance to bunt and field.

DURATION: 12–15 minutes

5. GAME SITUATION BUNTING

This drill teaches bunting and defending the bunt. To set up this drill, divide your team in half. One way to do this is to put all your starting defensive players in the infield. The other half of the team is at bat and on base. If you cannot cover all positions in the field, make sure the infield positions are covered. The coach pitches from the mound. Start with a runner at first base and a hitter at home plate.

The first baseman handles all balls bunted between the mound and the first base foul line. The second baseman covers first base when the first baseman handles the bunt. The shortstop covers second base. The third baseman handles all balls bunted between the mound and the third base foul line. The catcher is responsible for covering third when the third baseman gets the ball. The pitcher handles all balls bunted toward the mound area.

To run the drill, the coach pitches and the hitter bunts toward first or third, 12 to 15 feet down either foul line. The catcher directs the throw from the fielded bunt by calling out, "One, one, one" if the ball is to be thrown to first base and "Two, two, two" if the ball is to be thrown to second base. The outfielders move to their correct backup positions once the bunt is in play. The baserunner reacts to the bunted ball, only advancing to second when he sees the ball is on the ground. The bunter sprints hard to first base to put pressure on any throws in that direction. Once the runner on first gets to second, he returns home, outside the foul line, and a new hitter sets up to bunt. Once every player on the hitting team gets a chance to bunt, that half of the team changes positions with the fielders. The fielders now have a chance to bunt, and the hitters have a chance to field.

DURATION: 10–15 minutes

Games

1. TARGET

For this game, divide your players into two teams. Each team gets one at bat. Put a cone close to the first and third baselines, somewhere between 12 and 15 feet from home. The coach pitches to each player twice. Players bunt, trying to hit the cone on either baseline. Any time a player hits the cone with his bunt, his team gets one point. The team with the most points wins.

DURATION: 8 minutes

PART III

ESSENTIAL INFORMATION

CHAPTER 11

IMPROVING AS A COACH

The only problem with success is that it does not teach you about failure.
—Tommy Lasorda

You already have more working knowledge of baseball than your players. Master the fundamentals you learned in this book, and you will be well on your way to making a huge impact as a coach. Baseball is a simple game; keep it simple. A great coach is a great teacher. Teach and encourage constantly.

The goal for every coach at every level should be continual growth. There is a wealth of knowledge out there for aspiring coaches at any level. Videos and tapes abound, and clinics are held regularly, especially in the off-season. A great resource is your local high school coach. In reality, you are the farm system for his program. Don't hesitate to ask him for some help with drills and with teaching the skills you are trying to instill in your players. Ask league officials to sponsor a teaching clinic for coaches with outside speakers prior to the season.

Watching professional baseball on television can be invaluable. Note the techniques of the pitchers, hitters, and fielders. Keep a journal on what you observe. Tape the game and watch certain areas in slow motion. Edit parts of the game that you are trying to emphasize with your team. Keep a library of your baseball references and refer to it. Your knowledge and enjoyment of the game will increase exponentially.

Have a file for handouts from the league and another for any handouts you give your players or the parents. Get an organizational calendar to plan out the weeks of the season you will be coaching. Use it to plan out your weekly tasks.

Buckminster Fuller once wrote, "Humans have learned only through mistakes." Don't be afraid to make mistakes, and learn from them.

Here is a suggested checklist of tasks for taking care of your team.

League rules governing games/roster sizes/playing time

Roster of league administrators/other coaches

League meetings

Team roster and contact information for players

Emergency procedures/medical kit

Practice and game schedules, including policies for rain-outs

Team rules: attendance, playing time, attitude expected

Uniforms

Equipment inventory/replacement policies/daily storage

Practice planning

Fundraising duties

Parent communication/handling complaints

End-of-year social

As a youth baseball coach, you will help your players develop a love for the game that could last a lifetime. Being on the field should be a highlight of their day—and yours. Over the course of a season, you'll be teaching skills, both on the field and off, that will truly stay with them for life.

BASIC RULES OF BASEBALL

*It's pitching, hitting and defense that wins. Any two can win. All three make
you unbeatable.*

    —Joe Garagiola

The Objective

The objective of baseball is for one team to score more *runs* than the
other team. The game is played for a set number of *innings* which change
depending upon the age of the players. A major league game is nine
innings. Each inning, each team takes a turn offensively and defensively.
The offensive team is *at bat* hitting the baseball thrown by the pitcher of
the defensive team and running all the *bases* consecutively to score *runs*.
The defensive team is in the *infield* and *outfield* retrieving the ball as
quickly as possible so runs cannot be scored.

The Play

The game is played on a field with four *bases* marking the *diamond*. The
lines from home plate through first base and home plate through third
base mark fair and foul territory. *Foul territory* is outside these base lines.
Fair territory is inside these lines.

    At the start of play, the ball is thrown from the *pitching mound* by
the *pitcher* to the *batter* at *home plate*. All *fielders* other than the *catcher*
must be in fair territory at this time. For a pitch to be called a *strike* by
the *umpire*, the game official who stands behind the catcher, it must be

thrown in the *strike zone*. The strike zone is the area over home plate between the player's armpits and the top of his knees. If the pitcher throws a ball in this defined area, and the batter does not hit it, this is a *strike*. If a pitcher gets three strikes on a batter, that batter is *out*. If the pitcher throws a pitch outside the strike zone and the batter doesn't swing, this is a *ball*. If the pitcher throws four balls on a batter, that batter *walks* to first, and other runners on base *advance* one base also. If the batter is hit by a pitched ball, he advances to first base.

Once the ball is hit into the air as a *fly ball*, if the defensive team catches it before it touches the ground, the player who hit that ball is *out*. For balls on the ground, the defensive team gets the ball and attempts to tag the runner with the ball or tag a base with the ball before the *runner* arrives. If they do this, this is also an out. Once an offensive player is out, he is done with his turn at bat, cannot score a run, and leaves the diamond. The team that starts the inning on defense is the *home team*. Once they make three outs, they are up at bat until the other team gets them out three times.

Batters bat in set order. To score a run, the runner must advance by touching first, second, third, and home plate in order. The runner cannot advance if the defensive team catches a ball that is hit before it touches the ground. The runner is then only safe once he has returned to the base he came from; until then, he can be tagged out.

Two runners may not occupy a base. If the base is tagged with two runners on it, the runner following is out. [For a description of each defensive position, see Chapter 6 on Fielding.]

Fair and Foul Balls

A *fair ball* is a ball in play; a *foul ball* is dead and not in play. Generally two umpires, one behind home plate and one behind second base, call the balls fair or foul.

A fair ball is a batted ball that lands first in fair territory, or first touches a player in fair territory. If a fly ball lands in the infield between home and first base or home and third base and then bounces to foul territory without touching anyone, this is a foul ball. If a fly ball lands beyond first or third base in fair territory and then bounces out, it is a fair hit. A batted ball hitting any of the bases or the pitching rubber and bouncing into fair territory is considered a fair ball. A batted ball that hits the foul line is considered a fair ball. A batted ball that hits foul territory is a foul ball, and is considered a strike, unless it is the batter's last strike when it doesn't count and the batter gets another pitch. A catch in fair territory dropped in foul territory is considered a fair ball. A catch dropped in foul territory is considered a foul ball.

A batted ball that hits the base runner is considered a dead ball and the base runner is automatically out. A batted ball that hits the base umpire is considered a fair ball.

Automatic Advances

If the base runner makes contact with a fielder trying to field the ball, this is *obstruction*. The base runner is considered out and any other base runners must return to their original base. When the defensive player deliberately or inadvertently impedes the path of the base runner advancing to the next base, this is *interference*. The runner automatically advances to the next base.

If a ball is *overthrown* by the pitcher into an area where it leaves the baseball field, the base runner advances one base. On balls overthrown by position players, the base runner advances two bases.

Any false move by a pitcher in set position to deceive the base runner by disguising the pitching motion is a *balk*. If a balk is called by the umpire, all base runners advance one base.

GLOSSARY

backhand. Term for receiving balls in the area of the player's throwing hand.

backstop. The high fencing behind home plate.

bag. A base.

ball. A pitch that is outside the strike zone.

ball and glove together. The ball is clasped inside the throwing hand, which is inside the glove.

baseline. The straight line between two consecutive bases.

base on balls. When the batter goes to first base because the pitcher threw four balls to that player.

base path. The area within 3 feet of the baseline.

bases. Four locations marked by canvas bags—home plate, first, second, and third—that delineate the infield diamond.

batter's boxes. Squares on either side of home plate, to accommodate left-handed and right-handed batters, where the batter must stand to swing.

batting tee. Ball stand used to improve hitting by keeping the ball stationary.

bench. Seating located behind the base paths to first and third where players who are not currently in the game can sit.

blocking. When the catcher positions himself so the ball cannot get by him.

bullpen. An area in foul territory off the field of play where substitute pitchers may warm up.

bunt. Offensive play in which the grip on the bat is reconfigured to deaden the ball and tap it only a short distance to advance a runner.

catcher's box. The area behind home plate where the catcher is positioned before each pitch.

closed. This refers to a favorable body position, with the front shoulder turned inward for throwing, pitching, or hitting.

club head. Area of the bat with the largest circumference opposite the handle.

cock the bat. Bringing the bat back and up into launch position prior to swinging.

corner infielders. First baseman and third baseman.

crow hop. A shuffling of the feet in preparation to throw.

cutoff man. A defensive player who aligns himself between the ball and the next logical base to be thrown to in order to quicken the accurate return of the ball.

dead ball. When the ball's path dictates suspension of play.

defensive team. The team that is pitching, catching, and fielding.

double clutch. When a player begins to make a throw, then pulls back, then repeats the action to throw.

drag bunt. A bunt that includes footwork to speed the batter's exit from the batter's box.

dugout. Another name for the area where players sit when they are not currently in the game, generally referring to a partially open structure with a roof.

fair ball. A batted ball that settles in fair territory.

fair territory. The playing field between the foul lines.

fly ball. A batted ball that goes high in the air straight off a hit by the batter.

foul territory. The playing field outside the foul lines.

glove side. Term for receiving balls away from the middle of the player's body on the side of his glove.

glove tuck. When the glove hand is drawn in toward the chest area.

ground ball. A batted ball that bounces or rolls on the field.

home run. When a batter hits a ball and touches all the bases to return to home on that one hit.

infield. Diamond-shaped playing area outlined by the bases.

infielder. A player who occupies a position on the infield.

inning. The section of the game where each team gets a chance to be on offense and score runs, and on defense to make outs.

launch position. The position of the bat prior to the swing.

middle infielders. Second baseman and shortstop.

offensive team. The team at bat.

on-deck circle. An area near home plate but out of the playing area where the next player at bat can warm up.

open. This refers to an unfavorable body position, where the front shoulder is turned outward and away from the body, which compromises throwing, pitching, and hitting.

out. By the rules of the game, when a runner is retired from active play.

outfield. The area beyond the infield, extending to the outfield fences.

outfielder. A player who occupies a position in the outfield.

over-striding. When the pitcher lands his stride on the heel, rather than on the ball of his foot.

pitcher's mound. A pitching plate or raised mound at the center of the diamond where the pitcher stands to pitch.

pinky-to-pinky. Term for the position of the hands when catching a ball below the waist.

pitch. A ball thrown to the hitter by the pitcher.

poles. Vertical extensions in the outfield of the foul lines.

power line. When the body, head, chin, front shoulder, and hip are in a direct line to the throwing target.

reducing the field. Walking through game situations in an area that is smaller than the playing field.

relay. A succession of throws and catches.

round the bag. When the runner rounds the angle at the base for better positioning to advance to the next base.

rubber. Another name for the flat rectangular plate that may mark the pitcher's location in the center of the diamond.

run. When an offensive player advances from home plate through first, second, third, and back to home.

rushing the pitch. When the pitcher comes too far forward before releasing the ball.

safe. Declaration by the umpire that the runner made it to the base without being tagged out.

short-arming. Not fully extending the arm when throwing the ball.

soft toss. A hitting drill where a player hits into a fence or backstop to work on technique.

squeeze play. A bunt play where the hitter expects to be thrown out at first while enabling a runner on third to score a run.

stay on the ball. A term that refers to the hitter keeping his head and upper body on the same plane throughout the swing.

steal. When a runner advances to the next base while the pitcher is pitching the ball.

stride. The step the hitter takes as the pitched ball is coming toward him, or one the pitcher takes as he throws the ball.

strike. A pitch thrown in the designated area over home plate by the pitcher; a legal pitch.

strike zone. The area over home plate between the batter's armpits and the top of his knees where the pitched ball must come in to the batter.

tag. When a defensive player touches a base while holding the ball to get an offensive player out, or touches an offensive player with the ball or his glove with the ball inside to get the player out.

take the pitch. Coaching cue that means don't swing at the ball.

thumb-to-thumb. Term for position of hands catching a ball above the waist.

touch pitch. A pitch where getting the proper feel of the grip is especially critical and challenging.

tracking the ball. Hitter visually following the ball from the pitcher's hand to the point of contact with the bat or with the catcher's mitt.

umpire. A game official.

wrapping. (1) When the hitter allows the barrel of the bat to wrap the back of the head while in launch position, significantly lengthening the swing. **(2)** When the pitcher allows his hand to move toward the outside of the ball as the ball passes by his head.

INDEX

ABOUT THE AUTHORS

Fran O'Brien has dedicated his life to teaching and coaching. A graduate of Tufts University with a master's degree also from Tufts, he has been the head baseball coach and director of social studies at Randolph High School in Massachusetts, the head baseball coach and assistant athletic director at M.I.T. where he won the ECAC championship in 1993, the head baseball coach at Holy Cross college, and the head coach of the Harwich Mariners. His awards include Cape Cod League Manager of the Year, New England Coach of the Year, the Jack Butterfield Award for

Fran O'Brien and Kevin O'Brien coaching the Harwich Mariners in 1990.

Devotion to College Baseball, and the McDonough Award for the New England collegiate baseball coach who best exemplifies respect, dedication, and appreciation for the game of baseball. In 1989, he was inducted into the Massachusetts Baseball Coach's Hall of Fame.

Kevin O'Brien has followed a standout career playing baseball with a professional career coaching baseball. After being chosen an All–New England Player in college, he went on to become a Cape Cod League All-Star and to play professionally for the New York Yankees franchise. A graduate of Tufts University with a master's degree from the University of Massachusetts, he has coached baseball at Brandeis University and in the Cape Cod League for the Hyannis Mets and the Harwich Mariners. He is currently a professional scout for the Toronto Blue Jays, and the owner of Boston's Sweet Swing Hitting Academy.

Beverly Breton Carroll is a writer whose work, both nonfiction and fiction, has appeared in numerous magazines and newspapers throughout the United States. She is also the author of *The Confident Coach's Guide to Teaching Basketball,* written with her husband NBA coach and ESPN analyst John Carroll.

Matthew Viglianti is a Boston-based photographer who contributes regularly to several Massachusetts newspapers. His sports photography work has taken him as far afield as Torino, Italy, to photograph the 2006 Winter Olympic Games.